The Seduction Cookbook

THE
SEDUCTION
COOKBOOK

Culinary Creations for Lovers

DIANE BROWN

innova publishing, new york

innova publishing
37 West 20th Street, Suite 1108
New York, NY 10011

The Seduction Cookbook
LCCN: 2004114779
ISBN: 0974937363

Published by arrangement with iUniverse, Inc.

Design by Fritz Metsch
Illustrations by Kathryn Parise

Printed in the United States of America
1   3   5   7   9   10   8   6   4   2

To my mother,
who helped me discover the food-heart link.

I have perfumed my bed with myrrh,
aloes, and cinnamon.
Come let us take our fill of love until the morning;
Let us solace ourselves with loves.

Proverbs 7: 17–18

Contents

Foreword: The Seduction Cookbook

It was the umpteenth time we were compelled to leave the dining room table before I had served dessert. Groping, kissing, and undressing each other, it seemed the humble feast I'd prepared had inspired us. "What is it about eating together that gets us so excited?" I wondered, as a finger full of whipped cream from our forgotten dessert was offered to my lips, then kissed away.

Eating together is one of the most bonding experiences humans can share. Studies of aromas and arousal show that the scent of food provokes the steamiest response, the theory being that our distant ancestors congregated right after the hunt, where the chances were increased of finding a mate and procreating successfully. The visual beauty of food, with its shapes and colors, induce many other senses to react. Tastes that stimulate our palates also cause physical responses. The ritual of dining evokes romance. But without scientifically or culturally analyzing the body's response to food, I have found the repeated outcome: When I prepare a sumptuous meal for my significant other, we find ourselves making wild, passionate love to one another.

How can you work this culinary magic on your mate? *The Seduction Cookbook* delivers alluring menus and foods styled to fit your seduction method, whatever it might be. Would you like to test the powers of aphrodisiacs? Prepare a simple, yet inspiring, omelet for the morning after? Plan a tantalizing Valentine's Day menu? Sup on sensual finger foods? Serve a fireside late-night snack? *The Seduction Cookbook* offers tips and techniques for finding the way to your lover's heart with sensual foods.

Introduction: What is Seduction Cooking?

Cooking and seduction are delicious arts that involve head, hand, and heart. Great lovers are inspired by passion, as are great chefs. How can you excite your lover's appetite? With seduction cookery, defined by utilizing recipes that are easily prepared, allowing a cook to spend less time in the kitchen and more time enchanting a lover. By exploring foods that appeal sensually to sight, taste, smell, and touch. Through serving menus that turn a dining experience into a culinary orgy. Devising dishes that sate but don't stuff. By sharing foods that make you ravenous for more…food or sex!

Seductive foods make us feel energetic, provide a sense of well being, and increase stamina. Coincidentally, the foods long considered aphrodisiacs are those packed with vibrant freshness, visual evocations, heady aromas, and nutrients needed for peak sexual performance. Do aphrodisiacs really work? Well, not many have been proven scientifically, but remembering that a little imagination can go far in the art of seduction, serving these sexy foods with a provocative story tempts a lover just through the telling.

Above all, serving it forth with a sense of humor and a healthy sense of adventure will reap the greatest rewards. Be curious. Try new things. Get your hands dirty. Wear a blindfold. Be a human dish. Flirt. Dress up. Dress down. Don't wear anything at all…if all else fails, showing up naked with the dessert course should get things moving in the right direction!

Write a Sexy Invitation to Dine

Send a single rose with a handwritten message tied to it.

◆

Use a tube of lipstick to write on your lover's car window or bathroom mirror.

◆

Deliver a pair of sexy underwear with a request to wear it to dinner.

◆

Send a singing telegram—write your own lyrics to a popular tune.

◆

Write a message in a secret code that only your lover could crack.

◆

Transmit an electronic greeting card, writing your own lascivious prose.

◆

Cut out magazine headlines to fashion an anonymous ransom-style note.

◆

Make a box of handmade Erotic Fortune Cookies (see recipe) spelling out specifics
for your seduction dinner. Place a personal ad in the local newspaper.

Seductive Starters

GETTING WARMED UP

Warm things up or get wildly carried away with these alluring initiators. You could even make these seductive starters the highlight of your dining experience by preparing a buffet of luscious tidbits.

Design the stage for your evening of seduction. Dim the lights and fire up plenty of candles. Create exotic lighting by draping scarves over lamps. A log in the fireplace is sure to heat things no matter the season, or a sultry breeze wafting through sheer curtains on a warm night imparts an alluring atmosphere.

Set an elegant table with a simple floral arrangement to make a romantic statement. But don't limit yourself: A couch with cushy pillows and a low table set with a buffet of starters can be a comfortably sensual spot. Or better yet, skip the dining room table, place a tablecloth strewn with rose petals on your bed, and explore the delights of finger-friendly foods.

Plan the seduction: Start at least two hours before your lover arrives. Chop. Marinate. Puree. Mix. Wash. Cut. Breathe. Select your favorite bewitching music. Set the table. Relax.

Yield to the magic of aromas. Use candles scented with vanilla (relaxing) or cinnamon (exhilarating). The smells of cookery excite as well; pungent roasted garlic, peppery ginger, fragrant onions, spicy chiles . . . entering a room wafting with fragrance evokes sensual exultation.

What to drink with your seduction menu? Well, not too much. As Porter said in Shakespeare's *Macbeth*, alcohol "provokes the desire, but takes away the performance."

Lastly, practice empathy when cooking for a lover. Be sensitive to food aversions or allergies. Nothing spoils the moment like a cry of "Ugh! I hate asparagus," or a case of hives.

What a delicious way to inject Cupid's arrow. Let the seduction begin!

AHI TUNA CEVICHE WITH AVOCADO

*I*f the sight alone of the curvaceous avocado, reminiscent of a woman's body, doesn't stimulate, the buttery texture will rouse the palate. This dish offers a smorgasbord of sensual delights; smooth, salty, creamy, spicy, and luscious. If you like, you can scoop the ceviche from the avocado cups with tortilla chips.

¼ pound fresh ahi tuna (available in fresh fish markets)
Juice of one whole lime
2 tablespoons fresh orange juice
1 ripe Hass avocado
1 lime wedge

Kosher salt, to taste
1 teaspoon minced serrano chile
¼ tablespoon fresh ginger, grated
¼ red onion, diced
¼ red pepper, diced
1 tablespoon cilantro leaves, torn from stems

1. Cut ahi tuna into ¼ inch pieces and place in glass or ceramic bowl. Pour lime and orange juice over ahi tuna. Cover tightly and refrigerate one hour.

2. Cut avocado in half, remove pit and scoop out contents, leaving enough avocado in skin to form a bowl. Chop scooped contents into ¼ inch pieces and salt generously. Squeeze lime wedge over avocado to prevent oxidation.

3. Take ahi out of refrigerator and add remaining ingredients, mixing carefully by hand. Add more salt to taste. Scoop into avocado halves. Serve.

Surprise your passion partner with a "Double-Bubble-Bath and Love Bites". . . a bath overflowing with bubbles, a bottle of champagne, and some delectable nibbles to feed him or her.

ARTICHOKES WITH WARM VINAIGRETTE

*T*his prickly blossom is best consumed in the spring, Aphrodite's reigning season. Consider the artichoke to be the symbol of seduction itself: a slow peeling of leaves, each one yielding just a nibble of flesh…the anticipation of unveiling the inner core…the euphoric satisfaction of discovering the heart.

2 teaspoons salt
2 tablespoons olive oil
½ lemon
1 large artichoke or 2 medium
½ medium shallot, minced

1 tablespoon grainy mustard
1 pinch red chile flakes
Coarse black pepper to taste
¼ cup red-wine vinegar

1. Fill a small stockpot with water, and add salt and 1 tablespoon olive oil. Squeeze lemon juice into water and add squeezed rind. Remove tough outer leaves of artichokes. Add to water, cover and bring to a boil. Reduce to a simmer, and cook until leaves are easily removed and heart is tender when pierced with a knife, about 15 minutes. Drain in a colander, cut artichoke in half and remove inner choke with a spoon. Set aside.

2. Place one teaspoon olive oil in a small sauté pan over medium heat, add the chopped shallot and cook until soft, about 2 minutes. Remove from heat; add mustard, salt, chile flakes, and red-wine vinegar. Slowly whisk in remaining olive oil. Pour over reserved artichokes and serve immediately.

Create a sensual experience for your lover by offering a finger bowl scented with flower petals or a dampened towel that has been heated in the microwave and freshened with a squeeze of lemon.

SPICY BARBECUE CHICKEN IN LETTUCE CUPS

*T*ake chicken married with the blood pumping fire of chile powder, fresh cilantro (in ancient times a symbol of harmony in relationships), and onion (attributed to restoring virility). Then wrap it up in an easy to eat package of Bibb lettuce, and you've got a perfect dish for seductive al fresco dining.

1 whole skinless, boneless chicken breast
Salt and pepper to season
1 tablespoon olive oil
1 clove fresh garlic, minced
1 tablespoon cider vinegar
1 tablespoon Worcestershire sauce
1 teaspoon brown sugar

¼ teaspoon chili powder
1 pinch cayenne pepper
1 pinch allspice
2 tablespoons fresh cilantro, leaves removed from stems
¼ cup red onion, wedge cut
6 large Bibb lettuce leaves, cleaned and dried

1. Season the chicken breasts with salt and pepper and place under broiler until cooked through, for approximately 15 minutes. Or purchase precooked skinless, boneless chicken breasts. Cut cooked chicken into slivers.

2. Combine cider vinegar, Worcestershire sauce, brown sugar, chili powder, cayenne pepper, and allspice in a small bowl.

3. In a sauté pan, heat olive oil to a sizzle. Add garlic, and cook until lightly browned. Add pre-cooked slivers of chicken. Quickly toss with spice combination. Cool chicken mixture and hold in refrigerator.

4. Place chicken filling into Bibb lettuce cup. Top each cup with red onion slices and fresh cilantro leaves. Fold over into compact roll. Serve cold.

Forget the forks! Pack this one up for an outdoor concert or festival along with a selection of fruits, cheeses, and homemade cookies for finger-friendly fare, made even sexier when fed to each other!

CHILE LIME SHRIMP

*P*ods of chile contain capsaicin, a fiery chemical that causes the brain to produce endorphins, igniting a sense of well being and enlivening these fruits of Aphrodite. This is a perfect finger food to feed your lover.

½ tablespoon olive oil
1 clove garlic, minced
16 medium sized shelled, deveined shrimp, tails
*   intact*

1 tablespoon freshly grated ginger
1 teaspoon minced serrano chile
2 tablespoons fresh lime juice
1 tablespoon cilantro leaves

1. Heat olive oil in sauté pan to a sizzle over a medium flame. Add garlic and sauté until soft, for about 2 minutes. Add shrimp and cook until pink on one side, about 2 minutes.

2. Turn shrimp, add ginger and serrano chile. Cook shrimp until pink throughout, about 3 additional minutes. Add lime juice, toss with shrimp, and remove from flame. Serve immediately on two plates, garnishing with cilantro.

Rev things up with a "body shot" taken right from your lover's erogenous zone: a dash of salt on his neck, a quaff of tequila poured into a collarbone and a fresh lime wedge balanced on his shoulder to suck it down.

FENNEL, ARTICHOKE BOTTOM AND ASPARAGUS EMPANADAS

*F*ennel stimulates desire. Artichokes have a long reputed aphrodisiac quality; street vendors in Paris used to cry, "Artichokes, Artichokes! Heats the body and spirit!" Asparagus, as told in ancient manuals, produces considerable erotic effect, especially when heated in oil. These scrumptious little pockets will warm the cockles of a lover's heart.

1 tablespoon olive oil
¼ cup white onion, diced
1 shallot, chopped fine
1 small fennel bulb, diced

6 asparagus spears, cut into ½ inch pieces
6 artichoke bottoms, canned in oil, chopped
1 teaspoon fresh tarragon, chopped fine
1 package prepared croissant dough, 8 servings yield

1. In a sauté pan, heat olive oil to a sizzle over a medium-high heat. Add onion, shallot, fennel, and asparagus. Cook until tender. Add artichoke bottoms and tarragon, tossing ingredients lightly to incorporate. Remove from heat and cool.

2. Preheat oven to 350°. Roll out prepared croissant dough onto cutting board. Fill each section with one tablespoon of filling. Fold over and seal by pressing with fork tines. Bake for 15 minutes. Serve hot. Makes 8 bite-sized empanadas.

Intensify your lover's sense of flavor and fragrance by slipping a blindfold over her eyes, then coaxing her to deeply inhale the tempting aromas of the empanadas. Tease her into opening up for "just one bite." She'll certainly want more!

SPICY EDAMAME

*S*oybeans are packed with phosphorus, iron and protein, potent in their capacity to strengthen the body and enhance the sexual appetite. These beans are a simple delight, eaten with fingers straight from the pod. Don't forget to provide an empty bowl for discarded shells.

1 tablespoon pink peppercorns
1 tablespoon black peppercorns

1 tablespoon of kosher salt, plus more for cooking water
1 (1-lb) bag frozen edamame (soybeans in the pod)

1. In a spice grinder or peppermill, coarsely grind the pink peppercorns and black peppercorns. Mix with 1 tablespoon kosher salt. Bring a large saucepan of salted water to a boil. Drop the soybeans into the water and cook until tender, about 4 minutes.

2. Drain in a colander and pat dry with paper towels. Toss the soybeans with peppered salt to taste and serve. Serves 2-4.

Create a quick and easy Asian-themed evening by picking up some sushi from your favorite Japanese restaurant or specialty market and a bottle of cold sake. Great for those nights when you are feeling more like nooky than cooking!

ROASTED GARLIC HUMMUS

*H*ummus is made from garbanzo beans and is cited in *The Perfumed Garden* to give "a man the strength to pleasure a thousand women." Or perhaps they give a man the virility to pleasure one woman a thousand times? Serve with pita bread, raw snow peas, carrot sticks or a nimble finger.

1 12-ounce can garbanzo beans, drained
1 head roasted garlic
Juice of 1 lemon

2 tablespoons olive oil
Kosher salt and ground black pepper to taste

Squeeze the roasted garlic from each individual clove. Combine all ingredients in the bowl of a food processor and process until smooth. Serve at room temperature.

It's true what they say about garlic, if the two of you are eating it, you won't notice the effect in your breath. Still, if you're nervous about giving a too-fragrant kiss, nibble on a piece of fresh Italian parsley to freshen up.

LOVER'S PURSES

*D*im sum is loosely translated as "to touch the heart." Making these dumplings with your lover can be an intimate occasion; simply prepare the filling in advance and later roll into wonton wrappers side by side. Serve with Chinese beer and soy-ginger dipping sauce. Dine on pillows on the floor, and pop these delectable treats into one another's mouth.

FOR SCALLOP OR SHRIMP FILLING

4 ounces raw scallops or shrimp, coarsely chopped
4 whole canned water chestnuts, minced
1 teaspoon freshly grated ginger
1 teaspoon rice vinegar
1 clove garlic, minced
1 teaspoon nam pla *(Thai fish sauce)*

1 teaspoon sesame oil
1 large egg white, beaten
1 teaspoon sugar
1 pinch salt and freshly ground black pepper
1 medium scallion, greens and white portion chopped

Mix all ingredients and hold in the refrigerator for 30 minutes.

FOR CHICKEN FILLING

1 cup napa cabbage, finely shredded
1 teaspoon coarse salt
4 ounces lean ground chicken
1 shallot, minced

1 garlic clove, minced
1 tablespoon soy sauce
1 teaspoon toasted sesame seeds

Toss the cabbage and salt together in a colander and let sit until the cabbage wilts (approximately 20 minutes). Rinse the cabbage and squeeze dry. Mix with remaining ingredients.

TO MAKE THE LOVER'S PURSES

24 round wonton skins
Prepared filling mixture

Water to moisten wonton skins

1. Place one teaspoon of filling in the center of a wonton skin. Using a pastry brush, moisten edges with water and draw all sides to center, pinching together to form a "purse" shape.

2. In a large pot filled with boiling water, cook the purses until transparent, about 8-10 minutes. Remove from water with slotted spoon and serve immediately with Soy-Ginger Dipping Sauce.

SOY-GINGER DIPPING SAUCE

¼ cup soy sauce
¼ cup rice vinegar
2 teaspoons sugar
1 medium scallion, minced

1 tablespoon grated fresh ginger
1 teaspoon sesame oil
⅛ teaspoon chile flakes

Mix together all ingredients and refrigerate. Can be made 24 hours in advance.

Borrow some props from your favorite Chinese restaurant: Chopsticks are a fun and frisky way to feed each other, and those little white take-out boxes are a great way to wrap small gifts.

SWEET MELON WITH PROSCIUTTO

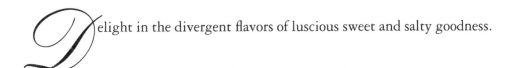

*D*elight in the divergent flavors of luscious sweet and salty goodness.

¼ cantaloupe or honeydew melon

1 ounce thinly sliced prosciutto

1. Cut each slice of prosciutto lengthwise into 3 strips.

2. Cut the ¼ melon section into quarters. Cut the skin of the melon from each wedge, and cut each wedge in half. Wrap one strip of prosciutto around each piece of melon. Serve.

Make your plates look truly romantic with a garnish of edible flowers like nasturtiums, lavender, lemon verbena, rose petals or squash blossoms. They can be purchased in specialty markets, farmer's markets or grown at home. Carefully wash edible flowers before serving them in case they have been sprayed with pesticides.

MUSSELS *MÉNAGE A* TROIS

*M*ussels have been considered aphrodisiacs since the medieval times, when the word "mussel" also meant vulva. Rich in phosphorus and calcium, mussels prepared in any one of the three ways suggested can provide a true boost to the libido. Don't be shy about using your fingers to remove the meat of the mussel from its shell. Serve as a sensual starter, or turn into a meal with a salad choice and Green Basmati Rice.

MUSSELS WITH WINE AND HERB SAUCE

A classic preparation for a staple seduction food. Sop up all the luscious juices with crusty French bread.

1 tablespoon butter
2 medium shallots, minced fine
1½ cups white wine
1 pinch red chile flakes

16 fresh mussels, with firmly closed shells, any variety
1 teaspoon fresh tarragon, removed from stem, chopped
1 tablespoon fresh Italian parsley, chopped

1. In a stockpot, melt ½ tablespoon butter until bubbling. Add shallots and cook until transparent and tender. Add white wine and bring to a gentle boil. Add chile flakes and mussels. Cook mussels until they just start to open, approximately 5 minutes.

2. Add tarragon and Italian parsley, and cover pot until mussels open completely, for approximately 5 more minutes. Stir in ½ tablespoon butter until melted. Serve with broth in a bowl with an additional empty bowl to discard shells.

"Love does not consist in gazing at each other, but looking outward in the same direction."
—ANTOINE DE SAINT-EXUPERY

MUSSELS WITH FENNEL, TOMATO AND SAFFRON

Saffron is a sexy spice that stimulates the senses with its pungent aroma and vibrant yellow-orange color. The Greeks believed that a woman who ate saffron for seven days could not resist a lover. That alone merits a try, with a message to your paramour that "this is my seventh day."

1 tablespoon olive oil
2 cloves garlic, minced fine
1 small fennel bulb, cleaned and cut into 8 wedges
1½ cups white wine

16 fresh mussels, with firmly closed shells, any variety
1 pinch saffron (powdered or crushed thread)
Coarse salt and freshly ground black pepper to taste
1 whole plum tomato, diced

1. In a stockpot, heat olive oil. Add garlic and fennel, sauté until cooked soft. Add white wine, saffron, and salt and pepper. Bring to a boil. Add mussels to white wine broth and cook until they just start to open, approximately 5 minutes.

2. Add diced plum tomatoes and cover pot until mussels are completely open, for approximately 3 more minutes. Serve immediately in a bowl with broth with an additional empty bowl for discarded shells.

GREEN CURRY MUSSELS

Rich with Thai flavors, these mussels will melt in your lover's mouth.

1 clove garlic, minced fine
1 tablespoon green curry paste (available in the Asian food section of well-stocked supermarkets)
Juice of one whole lime

1 15-ounce can pure coconut milk
16 fresh mussels, with firmly closed shells, any variety
2 tablespoons chopped fresh basil

1. In a stockpot, mix garlic, green curry paste, lime juice and coconut milk and bring to a gentle boil. Add mussels to curry broth and cook mussels until they just start to open, approximately 5 minutes.

2. Add basil, and continue to cook mussels until completely open, approximately 3 more minutes. Serve immediately in a bowl with broth, and an additional empty bowl for discarded shells.

OYSTERS WITH APPLE MIGNONETTE

*O*ysters, rich with lore. It was rumored that Casanova ate more than 50 raw oysters a day to boost his libido. Their aphrodisiac qualities could stem from the fact that they resemble the female genitalia, or from their sensual texture. Their most classic preparation is raw, on the half shell, when they are their most potent. Ask your fishmonger to shuck them the day you plan to serve them, retaining their liquor. Serve on a plate of crushed ice with lemon wedges. Or enhance their erotic proportion by pairing them with another food ripe with aphrodisiac legend, the apple.

12 medium oysters, your choice of variety
½ cup apple cider
3 tablespoons finely chopped tart apple, such as
*   Granny Smith or Pippen*
2 tablespoons finely chopped red pepper

1 whole shallot, finely chopped
1 tablespoon finely chopped parsley
1 tablespoon cider vinegar
Coarsely ground black pepper

1. Clean the oysters. Combine oysters and apple cider in a small saucepan and bring to a boil. Steam oysters, covered, over moderately high heat until they just open, about 4 minutes. Transfer to a plate after oysters have opened, reserve steaming liquid, and discard any unopened oysters. Chill oysters until cool, about 30 minutes.

2. While oysters are chilling, pour oyster steaming liquid though a paper towel-lined sieve into a bowl to remove any grit. Stir 2 tablespoons strained liquid together with remaining ingredients and salt to taste. Discard remaining strained liquid.

3. Remove flat half of oyster shell and loosen oyster with a sharp knife. Put oysters in rounded half of shell. Arrange on plates and spoon sauce over oysters.

When it comes to oysters, the more you slurp, the better it feels! Eat them right from the shell, holding from the hinged end and tilting it towards your lover's lips, making sure that he or she sucks all of the liquor and meat from the shell.

Scotch Bonnet Chile Blini with Lobster

*S*hellfish, considered to be the headiest aphrodisiac, contains phosphorus, an element said to spark erotic desire. Chiles provoke amore by stimulating the same physical effects of lovemaking: the body becomes heated, the pulse quickens, and the face flushes. These starters are eaten with fingers, and can easily slip into the lips of your lover.

MAKES 6 APPETIZERS

1 small egg beaten, use half
¼ cup milk
1 tablespoon, plus one teaspoon, melted butter
½ cup flour
1 teaspoon baking powder
¼ teaspoon salt
¼ Scotch bonnet, or habanero chile, minced fine (use gloves when handling chiles and avoid touching your skin and eyes)

2 large lobster claws, poached and shelled, (purchase prepared from local fish market) sliced into six portions
1½ ounces of crème fraiche (available in the dairy section of well-stocked supermarkets) or sour cream
1 tablespoon caviar of choice

1. Beat the milk, 1 tablespoon melted butter, and egg (use half) lightly in a mixing bowl. Mix the flour, baking powder, and salt together; add them to egg mixture, stirring just enough to dampen the flour. Mix in chile.

2. Heat a griddle over medium-high heat and spread remaining butter over surface. Pour a tablespoon of mixture onto griddle and cook until bubbles form on top. Turn and brown the other side. Hold at room temperature. Blini can be made 12 hours in advance. Cover until ready to serve.

3. Top each blini with ¼ teaspoon crème fraiche, 1 lobster claw slice, and a dab of the caviar. Serve immediately.

CARROT, FENNEL AND STAR ANISE SOUP

The ancient Romans thought that fertility was directly linked to what a person ate. Little wonder that they looked at the shape, color and flavor of foods to determine their power to influence sexuality. Hence, root vegetables became a symbol of strength to the libido. This root is matched with fennel, itself purported to provoke sexual vigor, for a flavor combination guaranteed to whet the carnal appetite.

1 tablespoon olive oil
1 clove garlic, minced fine
1 whole shallot, minced fine
½ cup prepared chicken broth
3 whole carrots, peeled and cut into 3 portions

1 small fennel bulb, greens removed, cleaned, cut into wedges
2 whole star anise cloves
1 tablespoon fresh thyme, chopped

1. In medium saucepot, heat olive oil to a sizzle. Cook garlic and shallot until softened, but not browned. Add chicken broth, carrots, fennel, star anise, and thyme. Cook on medium flame, boiling gently, for 30 minutes.

2. Remove star anise cloves from mixture. In blender or food processor, add the above mixture to bowl and process until smooth. Serve immediately, or store in refrigerator and reheat.

Don't be a fair-weather lover and abandon your sweetie when he or she gets the sniffles . . . taking care of a sickie is a heartfelt way to express your care and concern. A bowl of fragrant, hot soup is the quickest route to health, and back to nooky!

CURRIED CHICK PEA AND RED PEPPER SOUP

 hot and spicy soup that will lead to a hot and spicy physical state.

½ tablespoon olive oil
⅛ cup chopped white onion
1 small garlic clove, minced
1 teaspoon mild curry powder
1 teaspoon ground coriander, toasted

1 12-ounce can garbanzo beans, drained
1 12-ounce can chicken broth
Salt and coarse black pepper to taste
1 whole roasted red pepper, peeled and pureed
1 tablespoon fresh basil, cut into strips

1. In a small saucepan, heat olive oil to a sizzle and sauté onion and garlic over medium heat until soft. Add curry powder, coriander, chickpeas, chicken broth, salt and pepper. Cook over a medium flame for 20 minutes. Remove from heat and puree in batches in a food processor or blender.

2. Pour the chick pea soup into two serving bowls. Swirl red pepper puree into soup, and top each serving with ½ tablespoon basil. Serve immediately.

Picnics aren't solely a warm weather pleasure...create a romantic outdoor food-fest for the two of you on an isolated, overcast autumn beach or an outdoor skating rink. Just be sure to bring a blanket big enough for two and a thermos filled with hot soup.

Gazpacho d'Amour

Tomatoes are an aphrodisiac known as *pommes d' amour* or "love apples." Seduce your lover on a sultry summer evening with this classic chilled soup. Serve with a crusty loaf of bread and raw vegetable crudités.

1 roasted red bell pepper
1 cup canned tomato juice
⅛ cup red wine vinegar
1 tablespoon extra virgin olive oil
⅓ cup chopped white onion
⅓ cup coarsely chopped seedless cucumber

2 ripe plum tomatoes, cored, seeded and coarsely chopped
Salt and coarsely ground black pepper
1 dash hot sauce, such as Tabasco or Cholula
1 tablespoon chopped flat-leaf parsley
Optional: ½ ripe avocado, pitted, peeled and diced, for garnish

1. In a blender, puree the roasted peppers with tomato juice and pour into large bowl. Whisk in vinegar and olive oil.

2. Add onion, cucumber, and tomatoes to tomato juice mixture. Working in small batches, place the mixture into a blender or food processor and pulse until blended, but chunky.

3. Season with salt, pepper, and hot sauce. Stir in parsley. Refrigerate at least 6 hours. Serve chilled. Garnish with avocado if desired.

In the summertime, fill your picnic basket with fresh fruit, cheese, a loaf of bread, a bottle of wine, and a thermos of this chilled soup. Don't forget an oversized, thick blanket, a book of your favorite love poetry, a corkscrew and some insect repellent to keep the critters at bay.

MISO (HORNY) SOUP

*M*iso soup is a fermented soybean broth with restorative powers.

2 cups water
1 tablespoon sweet white miso (shiro-miso)
¼ teaspoon soy sauce

½ cup cubed silken (soft) tofu
1 small green onion, thinly sliced

1. Combine miso with ½ cup water and whisk together until miso dissolves. Add remaining water, soy sauce, and tofu. Heat broth over medium low flame (do not boil), for about seven minutes.

2. Divide into two serving bowls, sprinkle with onion and serve.

ROCKET SALAD WITH BLACK MISSION FIGS

*L*ooking for a sexy salad? This is your sure bet. Rocket is the English term for arugula, a peppery aromatic salad green. According to the ancients, rocket had the virtue of restoring vigor to the genitalia and was mentioned by the Roman poet Horace to be an aphrodisiac. Figs are symbolic of the male and female sex organs, with ancient roots in mythology linking to figures like Cleopatra and Dionysus. The addition of honey throws mythic magic into the mix, with its reputation as the nectar of Aphrodite.

1 shallot, chopped
1 teaspoon Dijon mustard
1 tablespoon balsamic vinegar
¼ teaspoon freshly ground black pepper
½ teaspoon honey

2 tablespoons extra-virgin olive oil
4 cups arugula, cleaned and torn into bite sized pieces
4 dried black Mission figs, cut into quarters
8 cherry tomatoes, cut in half

1. In blender or food processor, combine the shallot, Dijon mustard, balsamic vinegar, black pepper, and honey. Process until smooth and slowly add the olive oil until emulsified.

2. Toss arugula, figs, and tomatoes with honey balsamic vinaigrette. Serve immediately.

Loving a vegetarian doesn't mean that you'll be challenged finding the right foods for seduction. Start with a salad like this, and a delightful meatless pasta dish and you will have a very grateful omnivore at your dining table.

MANGO JICAMA CHOPPED SALAD

*T*he succulent essence of mango was once used as a topical application to the genitals in Hindu erotica to stimulate desire. Match that reputation with the nutty crunch of jicama, which like all roots is rumored to restore virility. Top all that lascivious action with the potent pumpkin seed, and you'll be climbing the walls.

1 tablespoon fresh lime juice

1 teaspoon honey

1 teaspoon sherry vinegar or red wine vinegar

2 tablespoons extra-virgin olive oil

Coarse salt and fresh ground black pepper to taste

1 cup peeled, chopped jicama (available in the produce department of well-stocked supermarkets)

½ fresh mango, pitted, peeled and cut into cubes

½ small seedless cucumber, peeled and cut into ½ inch cubes

2 cups romaine lettuce, cleaned and torn into bite sized pieces

2 tablespoons toasted and salted pumpkin seeds

1. With a wire whisk, combine lime juice, honey, and vinegar. Add oil in a slow stream, whisking until emulsified. Season with salt and pepper.

2. Toss together jicama, mango, cucumber, and romaine lettuce with dressing. Sprinkle pumpkin seeds on top of salad. Serve.

Chopping all the contents of this salad may make your lovers muscles a bit tight . . . spoil him or her with a relaxing shoulder massage.

RADICCHIO, ROSE PETAL AND POMEGRANATE SALAD

*T*his salad is exquisite on a Valentine's Day menu. Pomegranates are known in many cultures as a symbol of fecundity, as roses are a symbol of love.

*1 head radicchio, washed and torn into bite-sized
    pieces*
*Petals from a fully bloomed red or pink rose, washed
    and dried*
1 small pomegranate

2 tablespoons chopped toasted walnuts
2 tablespoons walnut oil
1 tablespoon red wine vinegar
1 tablespoon pomegranate juice
Salt and coarsely ground black pepper to taste

1. Cut the pomegranate in half, retaining the juices. Scoop the seeds from the pomegranate carefully and set aside.

2. In a small bowl, whisk walnut oil with vinegar and pomegranate juice, seasoning to taste.

3. Toss the radicchio, rose petals and walnuts gently with the vinaigrette. Divide salad onto two plates and sprinkle with pomegranate seeds. Serve.

Use any leftover rose petals to adorn your dining table, and complement the romance of your table setting with no less than a dozen votive candles.

ENDIVE, ORANGE AND FENNEL SALAD

*T*he *Kama Sutra* refers to fennel as such, "If ghee, honey, sugar, and liquorice in equal quantities, the juice of the fennel plant and milk are mixed together, the nectar is said to be holy, and provocative of sexual vigor." For another serving suggestion, you could make this simple, yet sumptuous, salad.

½ tablespoon orange juice
½ tablespoon rice wine vinegar
1 teaspoon honey
2 tablespoons extra virgin olive oil
Coarsely ground black pepper to taste

1 head Belgium endive, washed, dried and cut into
  2 inch pieces
1 small navel orange, peeled and cut into segments
½ small fennel bulb, washed, cut into ½ inch thick by
  2 inch long pieces

1. With a wire whisk, combine orange juice, vinegar, and honey. Add oil in a slow stream, whisking until emulsified. Season with pepper.

2. Toss together endive, orange segments, and fennel with the dressing. Divide onto two salad plates and serve.

Play some under-the-table games to tease and titillate your lover. Try knocking off a shoe with your foot and running your big toe along the arch of his or her foot.

Sexy Green Salad with Mustard-Herb Vinaigrette

 basic, sexy starter that partners well with many seduction dinners.

1 tablespoon rice wine vinegar
1 teaspoon Dijon mustard
1 tablespoon extra-virgin olive oil

1 tablespoon finely chopped fresh herbs such as dill,
parsley, chives and tarragon
½ head Boston lettuce (¼ pound), washed and dried
with leaves torn into bite-size pieces

1. Whisk together vinegar and mustard in large bowl, then add oil in a stream, whisking until emulsified. Season with salt and pepper and whisk in herbs.

2. Add lettuce and toss with vinaigrette. Serve.

Holding hands at the dinner table keeps you connected while you're enjoying your meal. Sit opposite one another and hold your mate's left hand while eating with your right, concentrating on not letting it go for any reason . . . hopefully, you won't need to use the pepper grinder!

The Main Event

SEDUCTION DINNERS

Eating with your lover can be a romantic occasion, a perfect event for dressing up in your best finery, breaking out the china and crystal and practicing your best manners. Utilizing the rituals of etiquette when sharing a meal can be a sensual, spellbinding act.

But some cultures create an extensive list of dining "dos and don'ts" that take some of the fun out of daring dining, ruling what is appropriate to eat with your fingers or what to order on a first date to avoid disasters like drips and splatters. Enjoying a meal with your lover should never be a repressive event. Be bold, spontaneous and creative in your own customs, remembering that a little culinary adventure builds sensual response. This is the time to tear down the walls of propriety.

Recall the ancients with their orgies replete with edibles and wantonness. Remember the celebrated *Kama Sutra* from India, which lists in its seventh chapter guidelines for attracting a mate utilizing aphrodisiac foodstuffs. Channel exotic erotica by trying a cuisine different to your own. Prepare a lavish, elaborate recipe. Make something quick and easy, savoring more time together. Eat the style of the triclinium, an antique Greek practice of arranging couches where diners reclined as they feasted on ready-served foods. Exchange sexy stories. Dress in erotic attire. Present a hot towel to your lover with orders that the meal will be eaten only with fingers. Or other body parts.

Prepare a scrumptious bite, gaze into your lover's eyes, and take an alluring mouthful. Give your fingers a brush of your lips. Watch your lover quiver in anticipation. Seductive Starters were the teasing "fork play" of the meal, and now you're ready for the real thing. The Main Event will awaken the erotic appetite of the ravenous lover.

SCALLOPS WITH ASPARAGUS AND GINGER BEURRE BLANC

*W*arm, succulent, silken scallops have a taste and consistency very appealing to lovers, and are rumored to promote friskiness. The speared heads of asparagus are a symbol of strength and in sixteenth-century folklore caused "the virile member to be on the alert, night and day." *The Perfumed Garden* said that a man should be able to "do it quicker than you can cook asparagus." Many aphrodisiacs were thought to have powers because of their shape being so similar to the phallus. The root ginger evokes a crude phallic symbol, but its pungent, spicy, mouth-watering flavor is what is truly provocative.

Serve with a buttery chardonnay and your choice of a Seductive Starter.

4 tablespoons cold butter, cut into ½ inch cubes
1 shallot, minced
1 tablespoon grated fresh ginger
½ cup dry white wine

Coarse salt and coarsely ground black pepper, to taste
10 medium fresh asparagus spears, trimmed
8 jumbo fresh sea scallops, sliced crosswise in half

1. In a sauté pan, heat ½ tablespoon butter over medium heat until bubbling. Add the shallot and ginger, cooking until shallot is soft, about 3 minutes. Add white wine and simmer until reduced by half, about 5 minutes. Cut 3 tablespoons cold butter into ½ inch cubes and add to wine sauce, incorporating with a wire whisk. Stir until sauce begins to thicken, and hold.

2. In another sauté pan, heat the remaining ½ tablespoon butter until bubbling. Add asparagus and season with salt and pepper to taste. Cook until slightly softened, for about 3 minutes, and remove. Season scallops lightly with salt and pepper on both sides. In same sauté pan, sear scallops at high heat for two minutes on each side. Remove from pan and place in the wine sauce, quickly turning over to coat scallops with sauce.

3. Arrange 5 asparagus spears in a fan on each plate. Top with 8 scallop halves, and divide remaining beurre blanc between two plates, pouring it over the scallops and asparagus. Serve.

SWORDFISH WITH ANISE SEED RUB
AND MANGO-BLACK PEPPER SAUCE

*M*ango, a sweet, lusty, juicy fruit, matched with black pepper, is credited with creating excitement by stimulating salivation. Accompany with a Mango Jicama Chopped Salad, Green Basmati Rice, and a California sauvignon blanc, and you've got a meal designed to make your mate restless.

1 cup dry white wine
2 tablespoons whole black peppercorns
1 tablespoon honey
½ ripe mango, cut into ½ inch chunks
½ teaspoon crushed anise seed

½ teaspoon coarsely ground black pepper
¼ teaspoon salt
1 tablespoon olive oil
2 8-ounce swordfish steaks
2 tablespoons fresh cilantro leaves, as garnish

1. In small saucepan, combine white wine, black peppercorns and honey. Bring to simmer and reduce until syrupy in consistency. Remove peppercorns. In a blender or food processor puree mango until smooth, and add the black pepper glaze.

2. Brush both sides of swordfish with olive oil. Season with crushed anise seed, salt and pepper. Heat grill or grill pan, and cook swordfish on each side, turning slightly to mark, about 4 minutes on each side. Pool the mango-black pepper sauce on two plates, place swordfish on top and garnish with cilantro. Serve.

Every seduction chef should have an apron . . . a fetching accessory, especially when nothing is worn beneath it!

CRAB OR SALMON CAKES WITH PINK GRAPEFRUIT SAUCE

*P*ucker up for this great taste sensation! Scrumptious with Garlic Mashed Potatoes and an Italian pinot grigio.

2 pink grapefruit, about 1 pound each
1 tablespoon finely diced red bell pepper
½ celery stalk, diced
1 green onion, white part only, chopped
½ tablespoon chopped parsley
1 large egg
¼ teaspoon dry mustard
Fresh ground black pepper, to taste
1 pinch cayenne pepper

¼ pound shelled cooked crab, or ¼ pound fresh salmon,
    coarsely chopped
About ½ cup dried bread crumbs, preferably Panko
    Japanese-style breadcrumbs
3 tablespoons butter
4 small white mushrooms, minced
¼ teaspoon fresh chopped thyme
¼ cup dry white wine
Chopped parsley for garnish

1. With a knife, cut peel and white membrane from one grapefruit. Holding fruit over a strainer nested in a bowl, cut between inner membrane and segments to release. Drop segments in strainer; save juice. Cut second grapefruit in half and juice by hand or with juicer into bowl with saved juice.

2. Put bread crumbs in a shallow pan. Form crab or salmon mixture into four cakes and coat with bread crumbs. Repeat with remaining mixture and place on waxed paper.

3. In a non-stick frying pan over medium heat, melt 2 tablespoons butter. When bubbling, set crab cakes in pan. Cook, turning once, until browned on both sides, 5 to 8 minutes total. Set cakes on plates and keep warm.

4. In a sauté pan, heat ½ tablespoon butter. Add mushrooms and stir over high heat until mushrooms begin to brown. Add thyme, white wine, and retained grapefruit juice. Boil over high heat, stirring occasionally, until reduced by half. Swirl in ½ tablespoon butter, and spoon around crab or salmon cakes. Garnish with grapefruit segments and chopped fresh parsley. Serve.

BAKED SALMON WITH RASPBERRY CABERNET SAUCE

The heavenly fragrance of this sauce is an alluring prelude to dinner. Robust cabernet sauvignon and sweet-tart raspberries are well married with the rich flavor of salmon. For a dramatic and savory presentation, serve this dish with Roasted Beets and Sautéed Red Cabbage. The red visuals will make your lover's blood race.

1½ tablespoons butter
1 whole shallot, minced fine
2 cups cabernet sauvignon
1 teaspoon fresh lemon juice

1 tablespoon raspberry preserves
Coarse ground black pepper to taste
2 8-ounce salmon filets, skinless and boneless
6 fresh raspberries (optional)

1. Melt 1 tablespoon butter in sauté pan on medium heat; add minced shallots when butter starts to bubble. Cook shallots until tender. Add cabernet sauvignon and cook over low heat, uncovered, until reduced by half, for about 45 minutes. The sauce should be syrupy in texture. Add lemon juice to reduction. With a wire whisk, quickly incorporate raspberry preserves and butter. Hold away from heat.

2. Preheat oven to 450°. Season salmon filets with course black pepper. Place in a baking dish and cook for approximately 15 minutes, less if a medium rare doneness is preferred. Place salmon filet on plate, pour sauce over fish, forming pool on plate. Garnish each dish with 3 fresh raspberries. Serve.

Invite your date to help you stir the sauce, then slip up behind him, put your arms around his waist and give a few light kisses on his neck to get his blood racing even more!

Mahi Mahi with Papaya Pineapple Mint Salsa

*S*hake up a mai tai. Put on a grass skirt. Your partner will be dancing the hula after dining on this tropical dish.

Green Basmati Rice is a perfect accompaniment to this Main Event.

1 medium sized papaya, skinned, seeded and diced
1 cup diced fresh pineapple
2 tablespoons minced fresh mint leaves

Juice from ½ lime
½ teaspoon minced serrano chile pepper
2 8-ounce mahi mahi filets

1. In a small bowl, combine papaya, pineapple, mint leaves, lime juice, and serrano chile. Refrigerate for at least 30 minutes, but up to 24 hours.

2. Prepare grill for cooking or heat a grill pan over high heat until hot. Season mahi mahi with salt and pepper. Grill on each side about 3 minutes. Place on serving dish and top with salsa. Serve.

Seduce your partner, island-style. Conjure up a tropical setting by transforming your backyard or balcony into a paradise. Set up a hammock or lawn chairs, a potted palm, a string of Chinese lanterns and play some soft calypso or reggae music.

BAKED COD WITH SHITAKE MASHED POTATOES AND SHITAKE SAUCE

*C*omfort food to a sensual extreme, this one-dish meal will satiate your lover into submission.

6 small red rose potatoes
2 8-ounce cod fillets
2 tablespoons butter
1 small shallot, minced
6 fresh shitake mushrooms, sliced

1 teaspoon chopped fresh Italian parsley
Salt and black pepper to taste
1 cup unsalted chicken broth
¼ cup heavy cream

1. Place potatoes in a stockpot and add water to cover. Bring to a boil and cook potatoes until they can easily be pierced with a fork, about 20 minutes. Preheat oven to 350°. Season cod filets with salt and pepper and bake in a glass baking dish until flaky, about 12 minutes.

2. In sauté pan, over medium heat, heat butter until melted. Add shallots and cook until soft. Add shitake mushrooms and cook until heated through. Season with Italian parsley and salt and pepper to taste. Add chicken broth, stir and cook at a low simmer until reduced by one-third. Add heavy cream, stir, and cook at low simmer until reduced by one-third. Remove from heat and hold.

3. Drain potatoes and mash with a wire whisk. Add half of the sauce to the potatoes and mix well to incorporate; potatoes should be lumpy, not smooth. Divide mashed potatoes onto two serving dishes, topping each mound with a cod fillet. Drape remaining sauce over the fish and around the plate. Serve.

Tuck a love note into your lover's folded linen napkin for a surprise that will make her smile.

SEARED PEPPER AHI TUNA WITH CUCUMBER SALAD

Rumored to have stimulating qualities because of its phallic formation, the cucumber's sensual flavor and cool texture will excite all of the senses. The essences of Asia give the ahi tuna erotic appeal.

1 medium cucumber, peeled and sliced into thin round slices
¼ red onion, chopped
½ cup rice wine vinegar
2 tablespoons granulated sugar
1 tablespoon sesame seeds
2 8-ounce ahi tuna steaks, about 1 inch thick

1 teaspoon kosher salt
1 tablespoon coarsely cracked black pepper
1 teaspoon oriental sesame oil
1 tablespoon soy sauce
2 tablespoons dry sherry
1 tablespoon chopped green onions

1. Mix the cucumber, onion, vinegar, and sugar in medium sized bowl. Cover and marinate for 30 minutes in refrigerator. Top with sesame seeds when ready to serve.

2. Sprinkle tuna steaks on both sides with kosher salt and coarse black pepper, pressing gently to adhere. Heat sesame oil in a large nonstick skillet over high heat. Add tuna steaks and sear until brown outside and pink in center, about 2 minutes per side. Transfer tuna steaks to plates and keep warm.

3. Add soy sauce and sherry to same skillet. Reduce heat and simmer until mixture is slightly reduced, about 1 minute. Spoon sauce over tuna steaks. Sprinkle with green onions. Serve with cucumber salad.

Hot and racy under-the-table games: Ladies, pass him your panties in the middle of dinner!

AJO COLORADO OR FISH IN RED GARLIC BROTH

*T*antalize your lover with fragrant Mediterranean spices and tender sea bass.

1 cup water
2 small red rose potatoes, cut into cubes
2 plum tomatoes, peeled, seeded and cut into cubes
½ red bell pepper, seeded and cut into cubes
2 cloves garlic, minced
½ tablespoon paprika

Pinch of cayenne pepper
Pinch of dried cumin
One thread of saffron
1 teaspoon sherry vinegar
Salt and coarse ground pepper, to taste
2 8-ounce fillets of sea bass

1. Bring water to boil in a medium, lidded sauté pan. Add tomatoes, potatoes, and red bell pepper. Add garlic, paprika, cayenne pepper, cumin, saffron, vinegar, and salt and pepper. Cook covered, until potatoes are almost tender, about 20 minutes.

2. Season the sea bass with salt and pepper. Add the sea bass to the broth and simmer at medium heat until sea bass is cooked through, about 12 minutes. Pool broth and vegetables on serving dish and top with sea bass. Serve.

Dining room doesn't have a view? Create your own instant get-away by hanging oversized butcher paper on the wall, and with watercolors, paint a sunset, a Mediterranean ocean view or palm trees swaying in the breeze.

BAKED SOLE WITH BROWN BUTTER AND FRESH BASIL

A simple, yet courtly, preparation for one of Aphrodite's treasures of the sea. Dish this up with Sautéed Spinach with Golden Raisins.

2 6-ounce sole fillets
2 tablespoons butter
Salt and pepper to taste

2 tablespoons chopped fresh basil
2 lemon wedges

1. Preheat oven to 450°. Season sole with salt and pepper. Place in glass baking pan and cook to medium doneness, about 10 minutes.

2. In sauté pan, melt butter over medium flame. Cook while rapidly stirring until butter is a deep brown color.

3. Remove the sole from the oven and place on serving dish. Top with brown butter and basil. Serve with lemon wedges.

Use the K.I.S.S. method for cooking your romantic meal: Keep It Simple *and* Sexy! Stick to dishes that are easy to prepare and that you feel comfortable making. You could even go through a practice run before you invite your date over. Having a gentle case of nervous butterflies is sexy, but an anxiety attack due to making an over-elaborate dinner is not!

BROILED HALIBUT WITH ORANGE BASIL BUTTER AND SNOW PEAS

 titillating combination of stimulating ingredients that promises love at first bite. Delicious with Wild Aphrodite Rice.

2 tablespoons butter, softened
1 tablespoon fresh basil, finely chopped
1 teaspoon orange zest, finely chopped
1 teaspoon honey
Freshly ground black pepper, to taste

2 8-ounce halibut filets
½ teaspoon olive oil
1 cup julienne cut snow peas
¼ cup fresh orange segments

1. Add basil, orange zest, honey and pepper to butter, and incorporate with a fork. Press into two pats between plastic wrap and place in refrigerator for at least 30 minutes.

2. Heat broiler. Season halibut with salt and pepper. Place under broiler and cook for about 4 minutes on each side, until flaky but tender.

3. Heat olive oil in small sauté pan over medium heat. Cook snow peas until tender but crisp, about 3 minutes. Add orange segments and cook until just heated through, about 1 minute. Divide between two plates, place halibut on top of snow peas, and top each filet with a pat of orange basil butter. Serve.

More under-the-table games: Pay some attention to your lover's unique erogenous zone by holding her hand and gently stroking the super-sensitive skin between her thumb and finger. Lightly stroking her forearm is a sure way to send shivers up her spine as well.

Cumin Seed Crusted Scallops with Leek Sauce and Celery Root Puree

*A*romatic cumin seeds have long been credited as an erotic stimulus, as celery root was a means for whetting the appetite for love in eighteenth-century France. Enjoyed with succulent scallops and creamy leeks, your mate will lick the plate clean.

1 leek, cleaned, cut crosswise into ½-inch-thick slices
8 sea scallops, halved horizontally and patted dry
1 teaspoon cumin seeds
Salt and freshly ground black pepper, to taste
1 tablespoon virgin olive oil
2 tablespoons dry white wine

2 tablespoons water
¼ cup heavy cream
1 small celery root bulb, about 10 ounces, peeled, washed and cut into large cubes
2 tablespoons chicken stock
Salt and pepper to taste

1. Toss scallops with cumin seeds, salt and pepper. Heat ½ tablespoon oil in a nonstick skillet over high heat until hot, but not smoking, then sear scallops until golden, about 2 minutes on each side. Transfer to a plate with tongs and hold warm.

2. Heat remaining tablespoon of oil in skillet until hot, but not smoking. Sauté leeks with salt to taste, stirring until golden. Add wine and water, then simmer, covered, until leeks soften, about 3 minutes. Add cream and simmer, uncovered, until slightly thickened.

3. Place celery root in a stockpot and cover with salted water. Over high heat, bring to a boil. Reduce to medium heat and continue to cook until celery root is easily pierced with a fork, about 20 minutes. Drain in a colander and place in a blender cup. Add chicken stock, salt and pepper and puree until all chunks are removed and celery root is smooth.

4. Pool cream sauce with leeks on two plates and divide scallops, placing on top of sauce, between both plates. Serve with celery root puree.

Couples who cook together share more than just close proximity with one another. All of the sensual joys of cooking, the smells, sizzling sounds, beautiful food transformations, the melding of tastes that create a perfectly balanced flavor, are better shared with a partner.

Cornish Game Hens with Orange, Ginger and Soy Sauce

These game hens become "pornish" when dished up beside Rocket Salad with Dried Black Mission Figs, Cherry Tomatoes and Honey Balsamic Vinaigrette, Wild Aphrodite Rice, and Sugar Snap Peas with Pearl Onions, plus your choice of a delectable, debauching dessert. Use your fingers to get every morsel of succulent meat from the bone.

2 tablespoons orange marmalade
1 tablespoon chopped fresh ginger
1 tablespoon soy sauce

2 small (under one pound) Cornish game hens
Salt and pepper to taste

1. Preheat oven to 450°. In a small bowl, mix marmalade, ginger and soy sauce. Salt and pepper skin of hens. Cover skin of hens with half of the orange, ginger, and soy sauce mixture.

2. Cook uncovered, basting the hens with the remainder of sauce midway, for about 30 minutes or until juices run clear when skin is pierced with a fork. Serve.

Studies show that taking time to engage in each sense—touch, taste, sound, scent, and sight—will quickly kick-start your lust drive.

Gorgonzola Cheese and Walnut Stuffed
Chicken Breasts with Roasted Grapes

*A*n elegant, sensual meal, perfect for a special occasion. Start with a Sexy Green Salad with Mustard-Herb Vinaigrette and serve Broiled Plums with Lemon Sorbet for dessert. A zesty red zinfandel would be a great wine selection.

2 boneless, skinless chicken breasts, 6-ounces each
Salt and pepper to taste
½ tablespoon butter
1 large shallot, minced
1 garlic clove, minced
½ teaspoon chopped fresh thyme leaves

1 ounce Gorgonzola cheese, (about ¼ cup)
1 tablespoon coarsely chopped toasted walnuts
1 teaspoon dry sherry
1 tablespoon olive oil
½ cup red seedless grapes, stems removed and washed
½ cup green seedless grapes, stems removed and washed

1. Place each chicken breast on large sheet of plastic wrap, cover with second sheet, and pound with a meat mallet until ¼ inch thick.

2. Heat butter in medium skillet over low heat until melted. Add shallot and garlic, stirring occasionally until soft, about 5 minutes. Add thyme leaves and remove from heat. Stir in Gorgonzola, walnuts, and sherry. Hold the filling at room temperature.

3. Place breasts on work surface, season with salt and pepper. Top each breast with ½ of filling. Roll each breast into pinwheel and secure with a toothpick.

4. Heat oven to 400°. Heat olive oil in a sauté pan over medium high heat until shimmering. Add chicken breasts, seam side down, and cook until medium golden brown, about 2 minutes. Turn and cook until medium golden brown, for an additional two minutes on all sides. Place chicken rolls in baking pan, surround with grapes, place in oven, and bake until chicken is deep golden brown and grapes are soft, about 20 minutes.

5. Remove chicken breasts from baking pan and hold for five minutes. Cut chicken breasts into 5 medallions, divide on two plates, surround with roasted grapes, and serve at once.

Broiled Chicken Breasts with Fresh Rosemary, Lavender and Lemon Zest

*I*magine the fragrance of an Elizabethan garden and frolic in the lusty flavors. Up the allure by serving this with Sugar Snap Peas and Pearl Onions.

2 10-ounce bone-in, skin on, chicken breast halves
Salt and freshly ground black pepper
1 tablespoon minced fresh rosemary
1 tablespoon minced fresh lavender

1 clove minced garlic
1 teaspoon grated lemon zest
2 tablespoons fresh lemon juice
1 teaspoon extra-virgin olive oil

1. Combine rosemary, lavender, garlic, and lemon zest in a small bowl. Combine lemon juice and olive oil in a second small bowl.

2. Spread a portion of the dry rub under the loosened skin of the chicken breast, and make three slashes in the skin. Brush skin with lemon juice and olive oil mixture.

3. Heat broiler and adjust oven rack to lowest position under broiler flame. Place chicken breasts skin side down on the broiler rack.

4. Broil chicken on bottom rack until just beginning to brown, about 12 minutes. Using tongs, turn chicken skin side up and continue to broil for 10 more minutes. Place broiler pan on highest rack setting until skin begins to brown and crisp, about one minute. Serve.

Create anticipation for your evening together by conveying how thrilled you are about seeing your lover. Call and leave a voice mail message when you know he won't pick up saying, "I can't wait to see you tonight," or leave a note in his pocket with the message, "I'm so excited about our special night tonight."

HORSERADISH AND PECAN CRUSTED CHICKEN

The assertive flavor of horseradish will state exactly how strong you feel about your partner, as it is reputed to have a sexually stimulating merit. Serve this with Garlic Mashed Potatoes and a bold chardonnay.

2 8-ounce boneless chicken breasts with skin
1 teaspoon olive oil
Salt and pepper to taste
2 teaspoons Dijon mustard
¼ cup Panko Japanese-style bread crumbs

2 tablespoons freshly grated horseradish, or prepared
   horseradish
1 tablespoon chopped scallion
1 tablespoon toasted pecans, minced fine
½ teaspoon chopped fresh tarragon
1 small shallot, minced

1. Preheat oven to 400º. Rub chicken breasts with olive oil, season with salt and pepper, and spread Dijon mustard on skin. Place skin side up in a shallow glass baking dish.

2. In a medium bowl, combine Panko, horseradish, scallions, pecans, tarragon and shallot.

Mix together thoroughly and pat mixture onto the skin of each chicken breast.

3. Bake until cooked through, about 30 minutes. Loosely cover baking dish with aluminum foil if the crust browns more quickly than the chicken cooks. Serve.

The more often a couple cooks together, the more intimate and experienced they become. They can communicate without words: a glance becomes an unspoken request to pass the horseradish, a smile to conveys appreciation for beautifully chopped scallions, a touch indicates knowledge of the entrée almost being ready, and a squeeze shows your pleasure in the outcome of your cooking mastery.

INTIMATE CHICKEN PICCATA

*T*his dish is especially intimate because of its quick preparation time. Less time spent in the kitchen means more time to share with your lover. Serve it with angel hair pasta tossed in butter and freshly grated Parmesan cheese.

2 6-ounce chicken breasts, skinless and boneless,
   slightly pounded
2 tablespoons flour
Salt and coarsely ground black pepper to taste
1 teaspoon olive oil

1 cup sliced white mushrooms
1 whole lemon, seeded and juiced
1 cup white wine
1 tablespoon capers
1 teaspoon butter

1. Place chicken breasts under plastic wrap. Pound slightly with a meat mallet to uniform thickness. Cover with flour, salt and pepper.

2. In sauté pan over medium-high heat, heat olive oil to a sizzle. Place the chicken breasts in pan and cook until light golden brown. Remove from heat and hold.

3. Place mushrooms in same pan, cook until slightly softened. Add lemon juice and white wine. Simmer over medium heat until slightly reduced, about 5 minutes. Add capers and swirl in butter. Drape sauce over chicken breasts. Serve.

Make time for making love. Plan a quick meal you can make together, dividing up cooking, chopping, sauce making, and clean up, then use that extra time to be completely romantic. Better yet, skip the clean up and get right to the romance!

STEAK *AU POIVRE* WITH PINK PEPPERCORNS

*D*ivine on a Valentine's Day special menu, this exquisite, yet easy dish, can win the heart of any carnivore. Delicious with meaty Grilled Marinated Portobello Mushrooms, a glass of merlot, and your choice of a sexy starter.

1 tablespoon sweet (unsalted) butter
1 shallot, minced fine
¼ cup cooking sherry
1 tablespoon pink peppercorns

¼ cup heavy cream
1 tablespoon coarsely ground black pepper
1 pinch kosher salt
2 8-ounce filet mignon or sirloin steaks

1. Heat broiler. Season steaks with course black pepper and salt on both sides. Place steaks under broiler and cook for approximately three minutes on each side for medium rare doneness.

2. In a saucepan, melt butter until bubbling. Add minced shallots and cook until soft. Add sherry and pink peppercorns and reduce by half. Stir in cream, and simmer until sauce thickens.

3. Place steaks on serving dishes and top with the peppercorn sauce. Serve.

Lay on your strongest flirting skills while dining: Give your date your full attention with plenty of eye contact while you converse, touch your partner lightly on the shoulder or back of hand to let him know how interested you are.

LAMB CHOPS WITH COARSE-GRAIN MUSTARD

*I*n ancient times, a strong infusion of mustard seed was thought to be a powerful erotic stimulant. Increase the seduction quotient of this dish by serving it with Honey Roasted Belgium Endives and an Oregon Pinot Noir.

2 8-ounce (¾ inch thick) lamb chops
Salt and coarsely ground black pepper, to taste

2 tablespoons coarse-grain mustard

1. Prepare grill for cooking or heat a grill pan over high heat until hot. Season chops with salt and pepper.

2. Grill chops until undersides are browned, about 3 minutes, then turn over and spread browned sides with mustard. Grill about 3 minutes more for a medium rare doneness. Serve.

Feed your partner her entire meal, creating the perfect, lustful bite and delight in watching her carnal pleasure.

PORK TENDERLOIN WITH CHINESE FIVE-SPICE RUB AND MUSTARD SHERRY SAUCE

Chinese five-spice powder is a pungent mixture usually comprised of cinnamon, cloves, fennel seed, star anise and ginger, all significant spices to incite sensual indulgence.

Serve with Broccoli in Orange Chile Oil and Sweet Potato Oven Fries.

½ pound pork tenderloin medallions, cut into 6 rounds (each about ¾" thick)
1 tablespoon packaged Chinese five-spice powder
1 teaspoon olive oil

½ cup sherry
¼ cup soy sauce
1 tablespoon Dijon mustard
1 tablespoon honey

1. Sprinkle spice mixture over tenderloin slices, pressing to adhere. Heat olive oil in a skillet to sizzle on a medium high flame. Sear the pork, turning after about 5 minutes. Cook for an additional 5 minutes, or until pork is cooked through. Remove pork from pan and hold on serving plate, keeping warm with an aluminum foil tent.

2. In the same skillet, add sherry, soy sauce, mustard, and honey, stirring with a whisk. Bring to a simmer and cook until reduced by half.

3. Place three tenderloins on serving plate, top with sauce. Serve.

Another under-the-table game: Put your lover's bare foot in your lap and give her a sensual foot massage.

SAUSAGES IN RED WINE

*B*y serving this dish, you'll become a Spanish conquistador and your lover a very willing victim. Start the meal with some fresh, ripe sliced tomatoes drizzled with olive oil and seasoned with salt and pepper, accompany the sausages with Sweet Potato Oven Fries and a Spanish rioja.

1 tablespoon olive oil
¼ cup diced red onion
1 cup Spanish red wine
⅓ cup chicken stock or canned low sodium broth

¼ pound uncooked chorizo sausage
½ cup water
½ tablespoon butter
Salt and freshly ground black pepper

1. Heat ½ tablespoon olive oil in medium saucepan. Add the onion and cook until softened, about 3 minutes. Add the wine and boil until reduced by half, about 10 minutes. Add the chicken stock and boil until reduced by one-third.

2. Meanwhile, in a heavy skillet, heat ½ tablespoon olive oil. Add the sausages and cook over moderately high heat until browned, about 3 minutes per side. Add the water and bring to a boil. Reduce the heat to low, cover and simmer until the sausages are cooked through, about 15 minutes.

3. Bring the wine sauce to a boil. Remove from heat and swirl in butter. Arrange sausages on plate and top with sauce. Serve.

Candles in the kitchen do much more than create an alluring ambience; they actually can reduce the tears caused from cutting onions. Crying shouldn't be part of your seduction meal!

Pasta Puttanesca

*I*n small coastal towns of Italy, "ladies of pleasure" made fragrant sauces to lure sailors to their parlors. The name of the sauce for this pasta *puttanesca* is a derivation of *puttana*, meaning "whore" in Italian. When preparing this dish, imagine the lascivious aroma to be a siren's call.

Grilled bread perfumed with virgin olive oil and garlic, and a glass of Chianti would suit this dish well.

½ tablespoon extra-virgin olive oil
3 cloves garlic, thinly sliced
8 peeled and seeded plum tomatoes, about 1½ pounds total, cut into large pieces, juices retained, or one 28-ounce can whole tomatoes
10 pitted kalamata olives, coarsely chopped
1 tablespoon capers
3 anchovy filets, coarsely chopped

1 pinch red chile flakes
1 tablespoon chopped fresh Italian parsley
1 teaspoon dried oregano
Ground black pepper to taste
¼ cup arugula, rinsed and dried
Salt to taste
2 cups penne pasta
Grated Parmesan cheese to taste

1. In a saucepan, heat 1½ tablespoon olive oil over medium heat. Add sliced garlic and cook, stirring frequently, until soft, about 4 minutes. Stir in tomatoes with juices, kalamata olives, capers, anchovies, red chile flakes, Italian parsley, dried oregano and ground black pepper. Simmer on low heat for one hour. Add arugula 5 minutes before serving.

2. Fill a large stockpot with water and season with salt. Bring water to a rolling boil and add penne pasta. Cook until al dente, tender but still chewy, for about 12 minutes. Drain well in colander. Toss penne into sauce, mound onto two plates, and top with grated Parmesan cheese. Serve.

Wild Wild Mushroom Pasta

long with their alluring earthy sensuality, mushrooms contain phosphorus and potassium, both said to invigorate the libido.

1 tablespoon butter
1 tablespoon olive oil
1 garlic clove, minced
½ pound mixed wild mushrooms (shiitake, portobello, oyster, and chanterelle)
cleaned, stemmed, and thickly sliced

1 teaspoon finely chopped fresh rosemary
½ teaspoon fennel seeds, toasted
Freshly ground black pepper, to taste
½ pound penne pasta
¼ cup coarsely chopped basil
2 tablespoons freshly grated Parmesan cheese

1. In a large deep skillet, melt butter in heated olive oil. Add the garlic and cook over moderate heat until golden. Add the mushrooms, fennel seeds, rosemary and pepper and cook, stirring occasionally until the mushrooms are tender, about 15 minutes.

2. Meanwhile, cook the penne in a large pot of boiling salted water until tender but firm to the bite; drain well. Add the pasta to the mushrooms, adding the basil and cheese. Mound onto two plates and serve immediately, offering additional Parmesan if desired.

Get wild with a sexy story over dinner. Whether it's fantasy or a true tale, erotic talk definitely has the hottest aphrodisiac value.

Capellini with Basil Arugula Pesto

*H*orace, the first century Roman poet, wrote of arugula's peppery bite and its ability to strengthen the male member. Pine nuts are touted as aphrodisiacs that increase fertility, or more importantly, enhance the desire to make love. Their creamy nut taste soothes the palate, while the bright taste of basil stimulates the taste buds. Garlic, with its capacity to strengthen the libido, completes the amorous flavor combination.

¼ cup (packed) fresh basil leaves
¼ cup (packed) arugula
¼ cup toasted pine nuts
2 garlic cloves

¼ cup extra-virgin olive oil
¼ cup grated Parmesan cheese, plus two tablespoons
Salt and pepper to taste
8 ounces capellini, or angel hair, pasta

1. Blend first 4 ingredients in a food processor or blender until nuts are finely chopped. With machine running, gradually add oil, blending until almost smooth. Transfer pesto to a bowl and mix in ¼ cup cheese. Season to taste with salt and pepper.

2. Cook capellini in large pot of boiling salted water until tender, but firm to the bite, stirring occasionally. Drain, reserving ½ cup pasta water. Return pasta to pot. Add pesto and toss to coat, adding enough reserved water to form a thin sauce. Mound on two serving dishes, topping with remaining cheese.

Sure, a dozen roses are a romantic token to send your partner, but a fragrant herbal bouquet says so much more! Parsley is associated festivity, lavender symbolizes loyalty, rosemary means remembrance, peppermint is for warmth of feeling, basil is an ancient Roman love charm, and thyme indicates courage, strength, and activity.

RUSTIC FIRESIDE FRITTATA

*E*ntice your paramour with this simple, delicious dish. Pair this with Roasted Asparagus with Lemon and a California sauvignon blanc.

1 tablespoon olive oil
2 sliced red rose potatoes
1/4 red onion, cut into wedges
1 clove minced garlic
1/4 zucchini, sliced

1/4 yellow squash, sliced
1/4 teaspoon chopped fresh thyme
Coarsely ground black pepper, to taste
4 eggs
1/4 cup grated Gouda cheese

1. Preheat the broiler. Heat olive oil in a heavy skillet over a medium high-heat. Add potatoes, onions, and garlic. Cook, turning occasionally, until potatoes are lightly browned, about 7 minutes. Add zucchini and yellow squash and cook until tender but crisp, about 2 minutes. Season with thyme and pepper. Lower to medium-low heat.

2. In a medium bowl, beat eggs with a fork for about 20 strokes. Pour into the vegetable mixture, stirring to incorporate. Add cheese, cover and cook about 3 minutes until eggs set. Place under broiler to brown lightly, for about two minutes. Cut into wedges and serve.

For a more casual, but cozy, dining experience, sit in front of the fireplace with pillows and blankets. Don't have a fireplace? Create your own indoor picnic with a checkered tablecloth right on the living room floor.

Seduction
ON THE SIDE

Every part has a counter-part, every man his mate. Hot and cold. Male and female. Yin and yang. Compliments set in balance create harmony at the table and in the body. Create the perfect match for your seduction menu with these sexy side dishes, guaranteed to enhance your amorous dining experience.

SUGAR SNAP PEAS WITH PEARL ONIONS

*P*acked with vibrant sweetness and a satisfying bite, sugar snap peas are tasty raw or cooked. In *The Perfumed Garden,* Nefzawi boiled green peas with onion, ginger, and cinnamon to excite sexual vigor.

6 ounces pearl onions, root ends trimmed and cut with an X
2 whole scallions, white and green parts, chopped

¼ pound sugar snap peas, trimmed
¼ tablespoon unsalted butter, softened

1. Boil pearl onions in salted water for 15 minutes and strain in colander. Rinse under cold water, and then peel.

2. Cook sugar snap peas in a large pot of salted water for 1 minute. Add scallions and pearl onions and cook for 1 minute more. Drain and toss with butter, add salt and pepper to taste. Serve.

Roasted Asparagus with Lemon

*C*ooked to firm perfection, these spears are easily eaten with fingers.

1 tablespoon fresh lemon juice
1 teaspoon olive oil
¼ teaspoon lemon zest

12 asparagus spears, trimmed
Salt and coarsely ground black pepper to taste

1. Preheat oven to 450°. Mix lemon juice, oil and lemon zest in a glass baking dish. Add asparagus; turn to coat. Sprinkle with salt and pepper.

2. Roast asparagus until crisp and tender, turning occasionally, about 20 minutes. Serve immediately.

GREEN BEANS WITH ALMONDS AND BROWN BUTTER

*L*emon enlivens these delectable pods, highlighted with nutty goodness.

¼ pound green beans, stems removed
1 tablespoon butter
2 tablespoons chopped almonds, toasted

1 teaspoon lemon zest
1 teaspoon fresh lemon juice
Kosher salt and coarsely ground black pepper, to taste

1. Fill a medium pot with salted water and bring to a boil. Add green beans and cook for about 3 minutes, until crisp-tender. Drain and refresh under cold water.

2. Melt butter in a skillet over medium-high heat, stirring while butter foam subsides and the butter begins to brown. Lower heat and add green beans, almonds and lemon zest, tossing to coat with brown butter. Add lemon juice, salt and pepper. Serve.

Honey Roasted Belgian Endives

*I*t is said that in medieval Germany, women used endive as a love charm.

4 endives, cored
1 tablespoon butter
¼ cup water

Salt to taste
½ tablespoon honey
1 teaspoon fresh lemon juice

1. Rinse the endives under cold running water. Melt butter in a large skillet. Add the endives, water, salt, and sugar. Cover and cook over low heat, turning occasionally, until the endives are tender and caramelized, about one hour; add a bit of water if the endives look dry.

2. Sprinkle with the lemon juice and serve immediately.

BROCCOLI IN ORANGE CHILE OIL

*Z*esty and provocative.

1 tablespoon fresh orange juice
½ teaspoon sesame oil
½ teaspoon orange zest
1 garlic clove, thinly sliced

½ teaspoon fresh ginger
Pinch Chinese five-spice powder
Pinch red chile flakes
½ pound fresh broccoli, cleaned with stems removed

1. Mix together first seven ingredients in a sauté pan. Over medium heat, simmer until reduced and slightly syrupy in consistency, about 3 minutes.

2. Steam broccoli in a pan fitted with a steam rack for about 5 minutes. Spoon orange chile oil over broccoli and serve.

SAUTÉED SPINACH WITH GOLDEN RAISINS AND PINE NUTS

*R*ich in vitamins and minerals, spinach strengthens the body. The addition of golden raisins and toasted pine nuts fills the spirit with the longing to make love.

3 ounces spinach, washed and trimmed
1 teaspoon olive oil
¼ cup golden raisins

2 tablespoons toasted pine nuts
Salt and pepper to taste

In a medium skillet, heat olive oil to a sizzle over a medium flame. Add spinach, tossing quickly. When spinach is wilted, add raisins, pine nuts, salt and pepper, tossing to heat. Serve immediately.

GRILLED MARINATED PORTOBELLO MUSHROOMS

*S*ucculent, meaty 'shrooms, marinated in a magic love potion.

4 small whole fresh portobello mushrooms
1 whole garlic clove, minced fine
1 teaspoon fresh chopped thyme
¼ teaspoon coarse ground black pepper

¼ cup olive oil
¼ cup balsamic vinegar
1 tablespoon soy sauce

1. Clean mushrooms, trim stems, and place in self-sealing plastic bag. Mix together garlic, thyme, black pepper, olive oil, balsamic vinegar, and soy sauce. Pour mixture into bag with mushrooms; seal and marinate for at least 2 hours.

2. Preheat broiler. Place mushrooms under broiler and cook until soft, turning every 5 minutes for approximately 20 minutes. Serve whole or cut into finger-sized segments. Serve.

SAUTÉED RED CABBAGE

*C*abbage often appears in medieval aphrodisiac preparations as a meaningful ingredient.

1 tablespoon butter
½ small red onion, thinly sliced

¼ red cabbage, cored and very thinly sliced
Salt and pepper to taste

Melt butter over medium high heat. Add onion and cook until soft. Sauté cabbage, tossing with butter and salt and pepper until tender, but crisp. Serve.

ROASTED BEETS

*S*weet, earthy, and visually stimulating, this dish complements chicken, fish, meat or anything that matches crimson red.

2 large beets, about 2½ inches in diameter
½ tablespoon butter

1 tablespoon raspberry, red or balsamic vinegar
Salt and freshly ground black pepper

1. Heat oven to 400°. Wash beets gently, cut away tops and leave root end intact. Put beets in a roasting pan and cover with aluminum foil. Roast for 45-50 minutes or until beets are easily pierced with a fork. Remove from oven and let cool for 10 minutes.

2. Remove skins by briskly rubbing each beet with a paper towel. Remove remainder of top and root end. Cut beets into quarters. In a large sauté pan, combine butter and vinegar, bringing to a simmer. Add the beets and simmer for about 5 minutes, tossing the beets in the sauce. Add salt and pepper to taste. Serve.

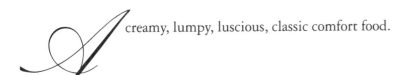

GARLIC MASHED POTATOES

A creamy, lumpy, luscious, classic comfort food.

5 medium red rose potatoes, skins on
1 garlic head, roasted
2 tablespoons butter

¼ cup heavy cream
Kosher salt and freshly ground pepper, to taste

1. In a stockpot, cover potatoes with water and bring to a boil over a high flame. Cook until potatoes are easily pierced with a fork but skin is still intact. Remove from heat and drain well in a colander.

2. Using a wire whisk, break potatoes into olive-sized chunks. Squeeze the roasted garlic cloves from their hull and add to the potatoes. Add butter, cream, salt and pepper, and incorporate with whisk, being careful to retain lumps of potatoes. Serve.

SWEET POTATO OVEN FRIES

*C*rispy terms of endearment.

1 large sweet potato, peeled and cut into ⅓ inch-thick by
3 inch-long sticks

1 tablespoon olive oil
Kosher salt and freshly ground black pepper to taste

Preheat oven to 450°. Toss sweet potato with olive oil and season with salt and pepper. Place on a cookie sheet, and bake until crisp, about 15 minutes. Serve.

WILD APHRODITE RICE

*I*t is said that when Aphrodite sprung from the ocean, the earth burst with fertility and abundance everywhere she stepped.

1 tablespoon olive oil
¼ cup celery, chopped into small pieces
1 large shallot, minced
1 cup water
½ cup wild rice
1 cup chicken broth
½ cup white rice

1 teaspoon dried marjoram
1 teaspoon dried thyme
¼ teaspoon dried sage
¼ cup dried apricots, julienne cut
¼ cup pecans, coarsely chopped
1 tablespoon orange zest

1. In small saucepot, heat olive oil to a sizzle. Sauté celery and shallot until soft. Add water and wild rice to sauce pot, and bring to a boil. Cover pot and cook rice mixture for 30 minutes.

2. Stir in chicken broth and white rice, and bring to a boil. Add spices and bring to simmer in covered pot for 20 minutes. Turn off heat; stir in pecans, apricots, and orange zest to rice mixture and let sit in covered pot for 10 minutes. Serve.

GREEN BASMATI RICE

*T*his blissfully fragrant rice enhances Thai-style and tropical menus.

1½ *cups water*
¾ *cup basmati rice*
3 scallions, white and green portions, chopped
1 garlic clove, minced

1 tablespoon chopped fresh cilantro
1 tablespoon chopped fresh Italian parsley
Kosher salt and freshly ground black pepper
to taste

Bring water to a boil over high heat in a small saucepan. Add rice, scallion, garlic, salt and pepper. Return to a boil, cover and reduce heat to low. Cook until rice is tender and liquid is absorbed, 12 to 15 minutes. Fluff rice with a fork and let stand, covered, for 5 minutes. Stir in herbs just before serving.

Sweet Seduction
DESSERTS FOR DEBAUCHERY

If Aphrodite reigns over all that springs from the sea and the fruits of the earth, then Eros, her son, surely rules over sweet seduction. With his pudgy knees, his gleeful grin, and his twinkling toes, he flies about with his golden arrow poised to take a shot at an unsuspecting lover. He is present to remind us of the intoxicating bewitchment of delicious dessert.

Enchanting chocolate, lush honey, magnificent berries, sugar-spun fruits, creamy custards—all of these are stuff of aphrodisiac myth.

Considering the rich erogenous merits of sweetmeats, one might even succumb to their sorcery by skipping a meal altogether. But think of them as the decadent icing on the cake, the applause after the performance, the Cupid's arrow of dinner.

These sweet seductions will deliver the golden glow of Eros' dart straight to the heart of your lover.

SUMPTUOUS STUFFED STRAWBERRIES WITH MASCARPONE CHEESE AND DARK CHOCOLATE

*S*trawberries are fantasy food for lovers: finger-amiable, juicy, and sweet. These stuffed strawberries are elevated to ambrosia with the addition of buttery-rich mascarpone cheese and pleasure-producing chocolate.

12 large strawberries
4 ounces mascarpone cheese
½ teaspoon super-fine granulated sugar

2 drops vanilla extract
2 tablespoons grated dark chocolate

1. Rinse and dry strawberries. With a paring knife, remove the hull and inner meat of the berry, forming a cavity in the berry. Cut the meat of berry from the hull, and save the green stem and hull.

2. Mix stuffing ingredients until incorporated. With a small teaspoon, stuff the cheese filling into the cavity of the berry, and place the retained hull on top of the mixture. Serve cold.

Make these ultra-sexy by dipping them in melted chocolate, then feeding them to your lover, offering to help clean up any drips or spills, of course.

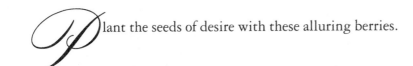

GOAT CHEESE, LEMON ZEST
AND POPPY SEED STUFFED STRAWBERRIES

*P*lant the seeds of desire with these alluring berries.

12 large strawberries
3 ounces goat cheese
1 tablespoon fresh lemon juice
1 tablespoon nonfat milk

½ teaspoon poppy seeds
1 teaspoon lemon zest
¼ teaspoon granulated sugar

1. Rinse and dry strawberries. With a paring knife, remove the hull and inner meat of the berry, forming a cavity in the berry. Cut the meat of berry from the hull, and save the green stem and hull.

2. Mix stuffing ingredients until incorporated. With a small teaspoon, stuff the cheese filling into the cavity of the berry, and place the retained hull on top of the mixture. Serve cold.

Why not begin your evening of seduction with dessert? Leave a note on the door asking him to meet you at the refrigerator, and wearing nothing but a sexy piece of lingerie, blindfold him while you feed him sweets a la *9½ Weeks*, in the luminous glow of the appliance lighting.

FROZEN GREEN AND RED GRAPES WITH SUGAR, LEMON ZEST AND WALNUTS

*G*rapes . . . the perfect finger food. Their sugar content gives a burst of energy, their package is easily eaten in bed as a prelude to love making. These babies ruled in ancient Greece and were associated with the god Dionysus, Patron of Fertility and Procreation.

1 cup sugar
1 tablespoon lemon zest
¼ cup whole walnuts
1 cup water

1 bunch (approximately ¼ pound) green grapes,
*   washed and removed from stems*
1 bunch (approximately ¼ pound) red grapes, washed
*   and removed from stems.*

1. In a food processor bowl mix lemon zest and walnuts; pulse to process into very fine particles. Combine with sugar.

2. Moisten grapes with water and roll in sugar mixture. Place on baking sheet and freeze for approximately 30 minutes or up to 24 hours.

In a Food in America Poll conducted by *Food & Wine Magazine* in 2003, 53% of people polled said that nothing is more romantic than when a woman hand-feeds a man grapes from a bunch.

WATERMELON GRANITA

*G*etting a little heated? Restore your lover with this cool delight.

2 cups ½-inch cubed seedless watermelon
⅛ cup sugar
½ tablespoon fresh lemon juice

1 pinch salt
2 strawberries, hulled and sliced, as garnish

1. Puree watermelon in a blender until smooth. Add sugar, lemon juice, and salt. Blend until mixed. Pour into small, metal baking pan. Freeze until icy at edge of pan, about 30 minutes.

2. Whisk mixture to distribute frozen portions evenly. Freeze again until solid, about three hours. Using a fork, scrape granita down length of pan, making icy flakes. Freeze again for at least one hour, or up to 24 hours.

3. Scoop icy flakes into two dessert dishes and serve. Top with a sliced strawberry.

Cooking outdoors can be very hot and sexy; desire starts to sizzle when you're working together side by side at the barbeque. Feed each other spoonfuls of this dessert when you're "grilling and chilling" on a sultry summer night.

POACHED PEARS IN CARDAMOM SYRUP

*E*rotic with their feminine shape, pears have a provocative flavor, texture and scent certain to lure your lover.

1 cup dry white wine
1 tablespoon honey
1 teaspoon chopped ginger

¼ teaspoon whole cardamom seeds
1 stick cinnamon
2 large Bosc or Anjou pears, firm, peeled, stem intact

In covered pot, combine white wine, cardamom seeds, cinnamon stick, ginger and honey. Place pears upright in pot; simmer on low flame for 30 minutes, or until pears yield to the pressure of a fork. Serve immediately, spooning additional wine sauce over pears.

Serve dessert in a sexy setting: your bathtub. Fill the tub with not-too-hot water, a few drops of an essential herbal oil like lavender and a handful of fresh herbs from your kitchen window box for a sensual after-dinner treat.

BROILED PLUMS WITH LEMON SORBET

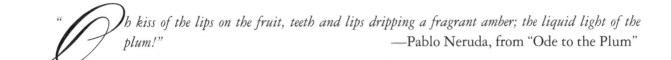

"*Oh kiss of the lips on the fruit, teeth and lips dripping a fragrant amber; the liquid light of the plum!*"
—Pablo Neruda, from "Ode to the Plum"

4 plums, halved
1 tablespoon sugar

Lemon sorbet

Sprinkle cut side of plums with sugar. Broil plums, sugar side up, in a shallow baking pan 3 inches away from heat until sugar is golden and plums are tender, about 3 to 5 minutes. Serve warm with a scoop of lemon sorbet.

Looking for a gift of romance that you can share, together? Skip the floral arrangement and deliver a basket of seriously sensual fruit. Pomegranates, plums, pears, figs, and mangoes are delicious choices. Feast on them after making love for a post-coital pick-me-up.

HONEYDEW WITH ROSEMARY SYRUP

*F*ortify your lover with the succulent honey of melon, highlighted with the romance of rosemary.

½ cup sweet white wine
1 sprig rosemary, plus two flowering tops of rosemary
*   for garnish*

1 tablespoon honey
1 tablespoon sugar
¼ honeydew melon, cut into slices

1. In a small saucepan, combine white wine with rosemary, honey and sugar. Bring to a gentle boil over medium heat and reduce by two-thirds until syrupy, for about 15 minutes.

Remove rosemary sprig, cool and refrigerate. Can be made up to 24 hours in advance.

2. Top honeydew slices with rosemary syrup, garnish with flowering tops of rosemary. Serve.

Bottle your own massage oil with a combination of essential oils, available at many health food and natural food stores. For a sultry blend, mix one ounce of jojoba oil, 6 drops of jasmine, and 6 drops of rosemary oil. Print a custom label with your own romantic message and instructions for use.

CARAMELIZED FIGS WITH RASPBERRY COULIS

*L*ike oysters, figs need little more to enhance their matchless sensuality. However, this preparation heightens the classic fig to a succulent dessert orgy.

5 ounces frozen raspberries in syrup, thawed
4 fresh figs, trimmed and halved lengthwise

1 teaspoon sugar

1. Force raspberries through a fine sieve into a bowl to remove seeds.

2. Preheat broiler. Sprinkle cut side of figs with sugar and place, sugared sides up, in a baking dish. Broil about 3 inches from heat until sugar is golden and figs are tender, about 3 to 5 minutes.

3. Divide raspberry coulis onto two dessert dishes. Arrange four fig halves on top and serve.

Raspberry coulis also has an exciting alternate use: as body paint! Make dessert out of one another by finger painting each other's bodies with chocolate syrup, caramel sauce, blueberry pie filling, and raspberry coulis. Cleaning up has never been so fun!

CHOCOLATE-DIPPED CHERRIES

*Y*our sweetheart will succumb to you when you offer these sweet little nuggets on their stem.

3 ounces bittersweet or semisweet chocolate, chopped

12 large fresh cherries with stems

1. Place chocolate in top of a double boiler set over simmering water, stir until melted and smooth. Remove chocolate from water.

2. Holding cherry stem, dip one cherry into chocolate. Place on a baking sheet lined with wax paper. Repeat with remaining cherries and chocolate. Chill until chocolate is firm, at least 15 minutes, as long as one day in advance. Serve.

Once a week, I spoil my sweetie with "Spa Night." I make homemade facial masks with a combination of one-half of a cucumber, a tablespoon of yogurt and three strawberries, whirled together in a food processor. We apply it on each other and feed sweets to one another while our masks dry. Then we head for the shower to wash off our masks and rub each other with a homemade ginger, honey, and vanilla sugar scrub: Combine 2 cups turbino sugar (raw brown sugar), 1 cup honey, 1 tablespoon vanilla essential oil, 1 tablespoon freshly grated ginger root. Combine the ingredients and slather on in the shower. Any remaining scrub will keep in the refrigerator for two weeks.

FRESH APPLE SLICES WITH
HOMEMADE CARAMEL SAUCE

*A*ncient Scandinavians thought apples to be the food of the gods, and ancient Greek and Roman lovers threw them to would-be lovers. In medieval Germany, apples were thought to excite amorous advances if soaked in the perspiration of a loved woman. I suggest drenching them in caramel, and offering them to the lips of a lover.

MAKES ONE CUP CARAMEL SAUCE

1 cup granulated sugar
¾ cup heavy cream
1 tablespoon butter

1 teaspoon freshly squeezed lemon juice
2 green apples (Granny Smith, Golden Delicious),
* cored, cut into slices*

1. Combine sugar and ¼ cup water in a medium saucepan; cook, without stirring, over medium heat until boiling. When sugar just begins to brown, swirl pan; cook until dark amber.

2. Remove from heat, and slowly add cream, stirring with a wooden spoon. Add butter and lemon juice and stir to combine. Store in refrigerator, re-warm when ready to serve. Using fingers, dip apple slices into caramel and serve immediately.

Variety is the spice of life! Eat dessert in an obscure place that you've never thought of before, like on the balcony, rooftop, fire escape, or on a blanket in the back yard under the stars.

SEDUCTIVE CHOCOLATE SOUFFLÉS

*C*hocolate contains phenylethylamine, the same pleasure-producing chemical released when we fall in love.

¼ cup sugar plus additional for coating gratin dishes
2 tablespoons all-purpose flour
1 tablespoon cold unsalted butter
½ cup milk

¼ ounce semisweet chocolate, chopped fine
1 large egg yolk
1 large egg white

1. Preheat oven to 400°. Butter two ¾ cup gratin dishes and coat with additional sugar, shaking out excess.

2. In a small bowl blend together 2 tablespoons sugar, flour, butter, and a pinch salt until mixture forms into small pellets.

3. In a small saucepan, bring milk to a boil and whisk in flour mixture and chocolate. Cook mixture over moderate heat, whisking until thickened, about 15 seconds and cool 30 seconds.

4. In a bowl, whisk yolk lightly and whisk into chocolate mixture. In another bowl, whisk whites with a pinch of salt until they hold soft peaks and whisk in remaining 2 tablespoons sugar, a little at a time, until meringue holds stiff peaks. Fold in remaining meringue gently but thoroughly.

5. Divide soufflé batter between gratin dishes and put on a baking sheet. Bake chocolate soufflés in middle of oven for 15 minutes or until puffed. Serve immediately.

Give your paramour a sexy, flavorful chocolate kiss. After taking a bite of soufflé, playfully French kiss your lover.

Romantic Rustic Apple Tartlets

*"*Stay me with flagons, comfort me with apples; for I am sick from love.*"*

—The Song of Solomon 2:5

½ cup all-purpose flour

1 teaspoon sugar

⅛ teaspoon salt

4 tablespoons (¼ stick) cold unsalted butter, cut
    into ½ inch pieces

2 ounces cold cream cheese, cut into ½ inch pieces

1 teaspoon fresh lemon juice

½ tablespoon ice water

2 small Granny Smith apples

1 tablespoon fresh lemon juice

⅛ cup plus 1 tablespoon sugar

⅛ teaspoon ground cinnamon

⅛ teaspoon freshly ground nutmeg

1 egg white, beaten lightly

1. In a food processor bowl fitted with a steel blade, pulse flour, sugar, and salt to combine. Add butter and cream cheese; pulse until mixture has small, pebble-like curds. Turn mixture into medium bowl.

2. Sprinkle lemon juice and ice water over mixture. With rubber spatula, use folding motion to evenly distribute water and lemon juice into flour mixture until dough holds together. Turn dough onto a clean, dry work surface; gather and gently press together into a ball, then flatten into a disk. Cut dough into 2 pieces, shaping each piece into a disk about 3 inches wide. Wrap each disk in plastic, and refrigerate until firm, about 30 minutes.

3. On a lightly floured surface, roll out the pastry dough portions into two eight-inch rounds. Transfer the rounds to a baking sheet.

4. Preheat the oven to 400°. Peel, core and cut apples into ¼-inch slices and toss with lemon, sugar, cinnamon, and nutmeg. Arrange the apple slices in a circular mound on top of the pastry dough, leaving a one-inch border. Fold the border up and over, fitting snugly over the apples.

5. Bake the tartlets until the crust is golden brown and the apples are tender, for about 30 minutes. Cool tartlets for 5 minutes and serve.

BEGUILING BERRY CRUMBLE

*L*overs praise berries of all kind. Who could resist a sweet nibble held up to longing lips? Innovate the sensual berry with a delicious brown sugar crumble, sure to tempt the heart of your lover.

The crumble can be baked up to 6 hours ahead and reheated before serving. Serve with vanilla ice cream or freshly whipped cream.

¼ cup plus 1 tablespoon brown sugar
⅛ cup all-purpose flour
⅛ cup rolled oats
¼ teaspoon cinnamon
Pinch of salt
2 tablespoons unsalted butter, cut into pieces

1 tablespoons fresh lemon juice
½ tablespoon cornstarch
⅛ teaspoon finely grated fresh ginger
1 cup mixed berries (blueberries, raspberries, boysen-berries)

1. Preheat oven to 400°. In a medium bowl, combine ¼ cup of the brown sugar with the flour, oats, cinnamon, and salt. Using your fingers, work in the butter until the mixture resembles peas.

2. In medium bowl, toss the berries with the lemon juice, cornstarch, ginger and the remaining tablespoon of brown sugar. Spoon the mixture into a one-quart baking dish. Sprinkle the crumble over the berries and bake for about 30 minutes, or until bubbling and the top is golden.

Kick-start an evening of passion by stimulating all of your senses: Savor the smell of the baked brown sugar as you remove this crumble from the oven, delight in the sight of the sumptuous blueberries, offer a taste to your lover, and with eyes closed, ask him to relish the sweetness in his mouth. Delicately brush your lips against his while his eyes are still closed.

CAPPUCCINO TIRAMISU

*T*ranslated from Italian as "a little pick me up," this ethereal dessert will make your lover tireless.

8 1-ounce ladyfingers
1 egg
¼ cup sugar
½ cup mascarpone, an Italian dessert cheese

1 teaspoon semi-sweet chocolate shavings, plus 2
    pinches for garnish
1 shot espresso or one demitasse cup very strong coffee
1 tablespoon coffee liquor

1. In a small bowl, beat egg and sugar, and then blend in mascarpone and chocolate until smooth and creamy. In another bowl, mix espresso and coffee liqueur.

2. In two large coffee cups, cappuccino mugs or small bowls, arrange ingredients in layers starting with 2 ladyfingers at the bottom, pouring ¼ of the coffee mixture over them. Place ¼ of the cheese mixture over the ladyfingers, and

2 more ladyfingers on top. Pour the remaining coffee mixture over the ladyfingers, and top each portion with the remaining cheese mixture. Sprinkle a pinch of chocolate shavings over each cup. Cover with plastic wrap and refrigerate for at least three hours. May be made 24 hours in advance.

3. Uncover tiramisu cups and serve chilled.

Enjoy a "body shot" strategically placed in one of your lover's most tempting erogenous zones, his or her belly button. Pour a small amount of amaretto, frangelico and a dollop of whipped cream, and indulge in *la dolce vida*.

Individual Gingerbread Cakes
with Honey CreamCheese Frosting

*I*n medieval times, small cakes were baked in ovens held over the naked body of a woman who wanted to ensure the affections of her lover. The warmth of the body was said to join with the heat of the oven to cause an inferno of passion when consumed by the object of a woman's attention.

FOR THE HONEY CREAM CHEESE FROSTING

2 ounces packaged cream cheese, room temperature

1½ tablespoons honey.

1. In the bowl of an electric mixer fitted with the paddle attachment, beat cream cheese on medium speed until light and fluffy, about 2 minutes.

2. Add honey, and beat until smooth, about 1 minute. Use immediately or refrigerate covered until needed, bringing to room temperature before using.

FOR THE GINGERBREAD CAKE

4 tablespoons (½ stick) butter, room temperature
½ cup sugar
1 egg
⅓ cup boiling water
⅓ cup molasses

1¼ cups flour
1 teaspoon baking soda
¼ teaspoon salt
1 teaspoon powdered ginger

1. Preheat oven to 350°. Butter and lightly flour two 3 by 6-inch mini-loaf bread pans.

2. Cream the butter, add the sugar, and beat until light. Add the egg and beat well. Add the

boiling water and molasses and blend. Mix together the flour, baking soda, salt and ginger, add to the first mixture, and combine thoroughly. Pour into the pans and bake for 35-45 minutes, until a toothpick comes out clean.

3. Cool in the pan for about 5 minutes, turn over onto serving plates, and spread honey cream cheese frosting over surface of each cake.

If you're feeling like an exhibitionist after dessert, do a sultry, seductive strip tease. Disrobe slowly, one piece of clothing at a time, showing just bits and parts of your skin. Duck under a throw before all of your clothes come off . . . this is a "tease" after all!

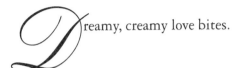

LAVENDER CRÈME BRÛLÉE

*D*reamy, creamy love bites.

1½ cups heavy cream
1 tablespoon dried lavender flower, or 2 tablespoons
  fresh
2 egg yolks

⅛ cup granulated white sugar
2 teaspoons granulated white sugar (to caramelize the
  crème brûlée tops)

1. Preheat oven to 300°. In a heavy-bottomed saucepan, bring the cream and lavender to a gentle boil. Remove from heat and allow the lavender to infuse with the cream for about 3 minutes.

2. Whisk the egg yolks with the sugar until light and creamy. Remove lavender from cream. Slowly pour the cream into the egg and sugar mixture, blending well.

3. Divide mixture between 2 ramekins or custard cups. Place them in a pan and carefully fill the pan with warm water, until it reaches halfway up the sides of the ramekins. Bake custards until set around the edges, but still loose in the center, about 40 to 50 minutes. Remove from oven and leave in the water bath until cooled. Remove cups from water bath and chill for at least 2 hours, or up to 2 days.

4. When ready to serve, sprinkle one teaspoon of sugar over each custard. Melt the sugar with a small hand-held torch or place under broiler. Rechill custards for a few minutes before serving.

Present your mate with a mock bill of payment:
Appetizer = One Shoulder Massage
Entrée = One Dozen Kisses (Location at your Discretion)
Dessert = One Long, Luxurious Foot Rub

Total = One Night of Sensual Love Making . . . Tipping is Encouraged!

EROTIC FORTUNE COOKIES

*F*irst, pen some sexy fortunes certain to make your lover's imagination go wild. You could suggest predictions for your lover's future, things you'd like to do for your lover, love quotes or a simple XOXO. Next, warm up your hooks for some fast-paced folding, as these cookies require adept preparation. Lastly, this recipe will yield 10 cookies, but be prepared to crack open only a few, depending upon how suggestive the fortunes are!

½ cup flour
1 tablespoon cornstarch
¼ cup sugar
2 tablespoons vegetable oil
1 egg white

3 drops vanilla or almond extract
1 tablespoon water
*10 sexy fortunes typed or handwritten on thick-bond
     paper, cut into ½ inch wide and 2 inches long.*

1. Heat oven to 300°. Combine dry ingredients in a medium-sized mixing bowl. Add liquid ingredients and stir until the batter is smooth.

2. Grease a non-stick cookie sheet with butter or non-stick vegetable spray. Drop one level teaspoon of batter onto the cookie sheet. Bake for 15 minutes or until cookies begin to brown lightly.

3. Remove cookie sheet from oven and remove one cookie with a wide spatula. Quickly place a fortune in the center, fold in half and press against the rim of a bowl to form fortune cookie crescent shape. Continue to shape the remainder of cookies, returning them back to the oven for 2 minutes if they become brittle. Cool and wrap in plastic or waxed paper. Can be made up to 24 hours in advance.

Here are some of my favorite fortunes:

Don't worry if we get into a lip lock, I've got the key ◆ *Hope you left room for dessert . . . I'm it* ◆ *Your lucky number is two . . . me and you* ◆ *Thou art to me a delicious torment* ◆ *The evening ahead holds many surprises, if you hold me first* ◆ *I have a secret; can I whisper in your ear?* ◆ *Kissing is like real estate, the most important thing is location, location, location*

SEXY FIVE-SPICE OATMEAL RAISIN COOKIES

*G*inger, cinnamon, long pepper, honey, and nutmeg compounded into a baked goodie are a specific Arab prescription for potency. In the Middle Ages, aphrodisiac spices were kneaded into pastries intended for the beloved. A little sugar and intensely flavored spice makes everything nice.

¾ cup all-purpose flour

1 teaspoon ground cinnamon

½ teaspoon freshly grated nutmeg

½ teaspoon ground ginger

Pinch cayenne pepper

Pinch ground cloves

¼ teaspoon baking soda

¼ teaspoon salt

1 stick (½ cup) unsalted butter, softened

½ cup granulated sugar

½ cup packed brown sugar

1 large egg

½ teaspoon vanilla

1½ cups old-fashioned or quick-cooking rolled oats

½ cup raisins

1. Preheat oven to 375°. In a mixing bowl, sift together flour, spices, baking soda, and salt. In a large bowl with an electric mixer, beat butter and sugars until light and fluffy. Beat in egg and vanilla. Add flour mixture and slowly beat until just combined well. Stir in rolled oats and raisins (dough will be stiff).

2. Working in batches, drop dough by level tablespoons about 2 inches apart onto an ungreased baking sheet and bake in middle of oven until golden, 8 to 10 minutes. Cool cookies on baking sheet for 1 minute and transfer to racks to cool completely. Makes about 25 cookies.

After dessert, slow dance with one another, holding each other tight and swaying to your own rhythm, even if there is no music playing.

Late Night
SEDUCTION SNACKS

A great night of dining and seduction can leave you hungry for more . . . food or sex! Be prepared for the moment your lover's erotic desire needs feeding with these swift, restorative snacks.

Peanut Butter, Banana and Honey
Sandwiches on Whole Wheat Bread

◆

Popsicles

◆

Kiwi Slices with Brie Cheese

◆

Cold Pasta

◆

Microwave Popcorn tossed in Cajun
or Curry Spices

◆

A Halved Pitted Avocado filled
with Pico de Gallo

◆

Toasted Sourdough Baguette Rubbed with Olive
Oil, Fresh Tomato, Topped with Sardines

Orange Segments and Strawberries Dipped
in Chocolate Syrup

◆

Pita Bread Stuffed with Diced Chicken,
Barbeque Sauce, Corn and Black Beans

◆

Leftover Soup

◆

Toasted Cinnamon Raisin Bread
with Cream Cheese

◆

Brie Quesadillas Topped with Heated Grapes

◆

Toasted English Muffins Mini Pizzas topped
with Pasta Sauce and Mozzarella Cheese

◆

Broiled Mushroom Caps with Bleu Cheese

The Morning After

BREAKFASTS TO REKINDLE
THE PASSION

Breakfast in bed. Hmm, sounds bucolic, lazy, and romantic. The Sunday paper, flannel pajamas, cartoons on television. How can you turn this torpid moment into a turbulent, torrid one? Rekindle the passion with these fortifying and frolicsome morning treats.

You'll want to serve breakfast without fuss. Prepare a tray with all the fixings ready to go into the frying pan. Set the automatic timer on the coffeemaker for an aromatic wake-up call. Or just whip up a "quickie"; a Seduction Smoothie or *Chai Masala* Tea with cinnamon toast is sufficient to sate and renew the sensual appetite.

Hang up a "Please Do Not Disturb" sign on your bedroom's doorknob. But don't limit yourselves to dine only in bed . . . the kitchen can be a hot spot for nookie too!

Restore your lover's sexual appetite with these temptations for the morning after.

The Perfect Omelet

y friend is convinced that preparing an omelet is a sure-fire way to impress a lover and nuzzle your way into his or her heart.

6 eggs

1 teaspoon butter

1. Crack eggs into a medium-sized mixing bowl. Beat lightly with a fork, for about 25 strokes.

2. Heat a seven to eight-inch well-seasoned heavy pan or nonstick skillet until a drop of water "dances" across the pan. Add butter; melt and swirl around the pan. Pour in eggs and let set slightly. With a wooden spatula, gently push aside the cooked eggs, allowing the uncooked eggs to distribute onto the pan's surface, cooking for about one minute.

3. Add choice of filling (see suggestions).

4. Before the eggs are completely set, shake the pan or use a spatula to loosen the omelet from the bottom and sides of the pan. Slide the omelet so that its edge lines up with the left edge of the pan. Using the spatula, roll the right third of the omelet over the middle third. Tilt the pan so that the left edge of the pan is touching the plate, then turn the pan over, folding the omelet out of the pan and over onto itself on the plate. Halve the omelet and serve on two plates.

Plan an entire day in bed, together, starting with breakfast and romantic movies, progressing to snacks and nooky poker (the "loser" has to perform a lascivious favor) and bringing in the evening with sensual music, a champagne toast and an easy supper.

SOME SEXY OMELET STUFFINGS

FINES HERBS: Whisk a tablespoon of fresh minced herbs, such as parsley, tarragon, or chives into the eggs before making the omelet.

SWISS CHEESE: Sprinkle ¼ cup Gruyere or Swiss cheese over omelet before folding.

SOUR CREAM AND CAVIAR: Salmon caviar creates a vivid, sensual presentation. Use 2 tablespoons of sour cream and 1 tablespoon of caviar before folding omelet.

SMOKED SALMON AND SOUR CREAM: Spread 2 tablespoons sour cream, ½ ounce of smoked salmon cut into strips, and one teaspoon of chopped scallions on inside of omelet before folding.

SPINACH AND PARMESAN: Sauté a minced shallot in one teaspoon melted butter until tender. Add a pinch of freshly grated nutmeg. Cook 4 cups (packed) spinach until wilted. Place inside omelet shell, top with 1 tablespoon grated Parmesan cheese, and fold omelet.

SUN-DRIED TOMATO AND BASIL: Fold one tablespoon of chopped sun-dried tomatoes and one tablespoon of chopped fresh basil into the eggs before making the omelet.

PICO DE GALLO: Toss together one diced tomato, 1 finely minced shallot, 1 tablespoon chopped fresh cilantro leaves, 1 tablespoon fresh lime juice, ½ tablespoon finely chopped serrano pepper and salt and pepper to taste. Place inside omelet shell and fold omelet.

MINT AND GOAT CHEESE: Chop 1 teaspoon fresh mint leaves and combine with two tablespoons soft goat cheese. Place inside omelet shell before folding.

JUEVOS SANTIAGO

*T*he consummate Latin lover created one of my favorite morning-after starters. These *juevos* will make your mate cry, "Bravo!"

6 eggs
1 tablespoon butter
½ cup pico de gallo, or bottled salsa

½ cup corn tortilla chips, slightly broken
½ ripe avocado, cut into thin slices
½ cup jack cheese

1. Crack eggs into medium mixing bowl. Lightly beat with a fork for about 25 strokes.

2. Preheat oven to 350°. Heat butter in a large skillet over medium high flame until bubbling. Add scrambled eggs and let set partially. Layer the tortilla chips, salsa, avocado and jack cheese on top of the eggs. Remove from flame and place skillet into oven.

3. Cook eggs until completely set and cheese is melted, about 7 minutes. Remove from oven and allow to settle for one minute. Cut into 6 wedges, place three wedges on each serving plate.

FOR THE PICO DE GALLO: Toss together one diced tomato, 1 finely minced shallot, 1 tablespoon chopped fresh cilantro leaves, 1 tablespoon fresh lime juice, ½ tablespoon finely chopped serrano pepper and salt and pepper to taste.

Getting away to a vacation home is an exciting way to spend the weekend with your honey. Dine out in the evenings, but create some vacation magic by serving a simple-to-make breakfast while you read the local paper in your pajamas together.

LOVE TOASTS WITH FRIED EGGS

simple yet significant gesture to convey your feelings on the morning after.

2 slices thick-sliced egg bread
2 large eggs

1 tablespoon butter
Salt and ground black pepper

1. Heat a large heavy-bottomed nonstick skillet over low heat for 5 minutes. Meanwhile, make a heart-shaped hole in each slice of bread, large enough to fit one egg, leaving crust intact. Add butter to skillet; let it melt and foam. When foam subsides, about one minute later, place bread in and toast on one side.

2. Turn toasted bread over and crack egg into heart-shaped hole in bread. Season egg with salt and pepper; cover and cook for about 2 minutes for runny yolks. Remove from skillet with spatula, slide onto plate carefully, and serve.

Another significant gesture? Remember exactly how your sweetie takes his or her coffee, and make a perfect cup. If she's not a coffee drinker? Win points by remembering her favorite morning beverage.

SCRAMBLED EGGS WITH WILD MUSHROOM HOME FRIES

*W*ild mushrooms conjure up images of inviting forests and frolicking fairies. These luxurious flavors will bewitch your lover.

2 large white or Yukon Gold potatoes, peeled, cut into 1-inch cubes
2 tablespoons butter
½ tablespoon extra-virgin olive oil

2 ounces fresh shiitake mushrooms, stemmed and quartered
2 ounces fresh oyster mushrooms, quartered
4 large eggs
2 tablespoons minced fresh parsley

1. Cook potatoes in large saucepan of boiling salted water until just tender, about 12 minutes. Drain potatoes, cool. Can be made one day in advance, held chilled and covered.

2. Melt one tablespoon butter with oil in heavy large skillet over medium-high heat. Add potatoes; sauté until golden, turning occasionally, about 15 minutes.

3. Melt ½ tablespoon butter in medium skillet over medium-high heat. Add the mushrooms and sauté until golden, about 6 minutes.

4. Crack open eggs into small bowl. Beat lightly with a fork, for about 25 strokes. Melt ½ tablespoon butter in medium non-stick skillet over medium-high heat. Pour the eggs in and move them around with a wooden spatula. Cook the eggs quickly, and do not over cook.

5. Add mushrooms and parsley to the potatoes, toss to combine. Season with salt and pepper. Serve with scrambled eggs.

Breakfast in bed is pure romance if you have all of the right equipment: invest in lap trays for two (perfect for a fast clean up, just put the trays in the hall a la room service style!), use tumblers instead of stemmed glassware to prevent spilling, light a few candles (even though the sun is already up!), and pick a single, fresh flower to adorn your lover's tray.

French Toast You Can Sink Your Teeth Into

*A*fter a terrific night of lovemaking, one can be as ravenous as a tiger. The most fitting breakfast is one that's decadent, filling, and a little bit naughty…breakfast you can sink your teeth into. Here's a simple French toast, best made with day-old sourdough slices and enjoyed with a simple cup of coffee (between the sheets).

2 large eggs
1 tablespoon whole milk
1 teaspoon ground cinnamon
¼ teaspoon vanilla extract
½ teaspoon granulated sugar

6 slices sourdough bread
2 tablespoons butter
1 tablespoon powdered sugar
Maple syrup as an accompaniment

1. In a medium sized bowl, combine eggs, milk, cinnamon, vanilla extract, and granulated sugar. Whip with a fork. Soak sourdough bread in egg mixture for 10 minutes, until completely saturated.

2. In a skillet, melt 1 tablespoon butter until bubbling. Place two slices of soaked sourdough bread and cook until golden brown. Turn and cook on other side. Remove from skillet. Continue to cook remaining sourdough slices in the same manner.

3. Place sourdough French toast slices on serving dish, top with remaining butter and powdered sugar. Serve with syrup.

Coffee itself is said to be an aphrodisiac, most likely because of its heady aroma and stimulating caffeine content. Make the best coffee possible by using freshly ground whole beans, and use a French press pot for a romantic presentation.

Banana Pancakes with Caramelized Walnuts

*W*hether it's their phallic shape or high potassium content, bananas are a whimsical aphrodisiac.

FOR THE WALNUTS

½ cup walnuts, broken into small pieces
1 teaspoon melted butter

1 tablespoon brown sugar
1 pinch cinnamon

FOR THE CARAMELIZED BANANAS

1 whole banana, peeled and cut into ¼ inch round
    slices

1 tablespoon brown sugar

FOR THE BANANA PANCAKES

¼ cup milk
1 tablespoon melted butter
½ very ripe banana, mashed with a fork into small
    chunks
1 egg
½ teaspoon vanilla extract

½ cup flour
1 teaspoon baking powder
1 tablespoon sugar
1 pinch salt
Maple syrup as an accompaniment

Treat your bedroom like a romantic hideaway for two; does yours stand up to a lover's holiday? Don't have a big screen TV blaring if you want to keep it sexy and sensual. Don't have a distracting computer. Do have mood-enhancing lighting, candles and flowers, soft curtains, and the best sheets you can afford.

1. Mix the melted butter, brown sugar and walnuts. Place on a baking sheet and under broiler, shaking frequently until sugar caramelizes, for about 3 minutes.

2. Place the banana slices on a baking sheet, sprinkle brown sugar, and place under broiler until sugar caramelizes and bananas are soft.

3. Beat the milk, butter, vanilla, banana and egg lightly in a mixing bowl. Mix the flour, baking powder, sugar, and salt and add them all at once to the first mixture, stirring just enough to dampen the flour.

4. Lightly butter or grease a skillet and set over moderate heat. Pour about ¼ of the mixture to form one pancake. Bake in skillet until the cakes are full of bubbles on the top and the undersides are lightly browned. Turn with a spatula and brown the other side.

5. Place cakes on plate, top with caramelized walnuts and bananas. Makes four large cakes. Serve with maple syrup.

RICOTTA HOT CAKES WITH STRAWBERRY TOPPING

*T*hese fluffy, creamy hot cakes topped with strawberries in their natural juices are perfect for pillow talk.

12 whole strawberries, hulled and sliced
½ cup sugar
1 large egg, separated
½ cup ricotta cheese
¼ cup all purpose flour

½ teaspoon baking powder
⅛ teaspoon salt
⅛ teaspoon baking soda
½ cup whole milk
1 teaspoon melted butter

1. In a small bowl, mix together the strawberries and sugar. Cover and hold at room temperature for 30 minutes, until juices are released. Store in refrigerator until ready to serve, up to 12 hours. Serve at room temperature.

2. Whisk egg yolk and ricotta until blended. In another bowl, mix flour, baking powder, salt, and baking soda. Add flour mixture to yolk mixture and stir until combined. Stir in milk. In another bowl, beat egg white with a whisk until soft peaks form. Fold beaten egg white into batter.

3. Heat griddle or large skillet over medium heat and brush with butter. Working in batches, spoon 2 tablespoons batter onto griddle for each pancake. Cook until golden brown, about 3 minutes on each side. Serve with strawberry topping.

Use the ancient Chinese art of feng shui to enhance the romance in your bedroom. In order to inspire love, you need to focus on the "relationship corner," the back right hand corner as you walk in the door. By having matched pairs of accessories like candles, pillows, vases and lamps, you can increase your potential for pairing up with your mate.

MORNING GLORY MUFFINS

What could be more tantalizing than warm muffins in the morning? Especially these ones which have a bright citrus flavor flecked with restorative poppy seeds.

MAKES 6 LARGE MUFFINS

2 cups white flour
½ cup sugar, plus 1 tablespoon for muffin tops
1 tablespoon baking powder
½ teaspoon salt
1 egg, slightly beaten
½ cup buttermilk
¼ cup melted butter

2 tablespoons fresh lemon juice
2 tablespoons fresh orange juice, plus 1 tablespoon for muffin tops
1 tablespoon poppy seeds
¼ cup finely chopped dried apricots
1 teaspoon finely grated lemon zest
1 tablespoon finely grated orange zest

1. Preheat oven to 350°. Butter a six-compartment jumbo-muffin pan. In a large bowl, mix the flour, sugar, baking powder, and salt. Add the egg, buttermilk, butter, lemon juice, and orange juice stirring only enough to dampen the flour; the batter should not be smooth. Add the poppy seeds, apricots, lemon zest and orange zest, stirring only enough to incorporate.

2. Spoon batter into the muffin pan, filling each cup about three-quarters full. Bake for about 20–25 minutes, or until an inserted toothpick comes out clean. Remove from the muffin pan onto a cooking rack. Brush muffin tops with orange juice and sprinkle with sugar.

Bring breakfast to your lover, whether she's at home, at work or outdoors. Pack a basket of muffins, a few pieces of fabulously ripe fruit and a couple of travel mugs of coffee for a delightful morning surprise.

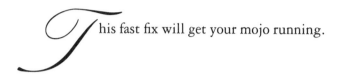

THE SEDUCTION SMOOTHIE

*T*his fast fix will get your mojo running.

1 cup mango juice
1 cup orange juice
6 strawberries, stems removed

1 banana
½ teaspoon grated fresh ginger
1 8-ounce container of lemon yogurt

Place ingredients in a blender cup. Blend until smooth and serve.

Couples who enjoy an active physical life together definitely have the stamina for more frequent nooky! Go for a walk, a bike ride, hike, or swim together and feel your libido lift!

ONE RIPE MANGO

*S*tart your lover's day with one ripe mango, peeled by your hand.

1. With a paring knife, cut off a slice from each side of a mango as close to the broad, flat pit as possible. Cradling the mango in your hand, skin side down, score long strips through the flesh, taking care not to cut through the skin. Turn the slice inside out so that the pieces stand up and separate. Cut these pieces from the skin.

2. Feast on this juicy fruit with all of your senses. Delight in its musk-like perfume. Savor its honey luscious essence. Feed a slice to your lover, rubbing the flesh against a lip or chin. Kiss the juice away and savor the salty sweet flavor.

3. Never use a silver utensil to eat a mango. The cool metal of a spoon will dull the taste buds. The best device for savoring a ripe mango is your loving hand.

CHAI MASALA TEA

*I*nfluenced by India, this sweet and spicy tea blend is certain to inspire. Serve with buttered cinnamon-raisin toast.

3 cups water
½ teaspoon ground cloves
¼ teaspoon ground ginger
⅛ teaspoon freshly ground black pepper
2 cardamom pods

1 cinnamon stick, broken into pieces
½ cup milk
2 tablespoons honey
2 tablespoons black tea, such as Darjeeling or Orange Pekoe

1. In small saucepan bring water and spices to a boil. Remove the pan from the heat, cover and let steep for 5 minutes.

2. Add the milk and honey to the pan and bring to a boil. Remove from heat and add tea. Cover and let steep for 3 minutes. Stir the *chai*, and then strain into two mugs.

Tea for two is a classic romantic and affectionate ritual. Use a beautiful china, porcelain or stoneware teapot to serve, and pour the tea for your lover. In many cultures it is considered bad luck to allow someone to pour their own tea.

More Morning After Quickies

A Broiled Grapefruit with Brown Sugar Glaze

◆

A Bowl of Beautiful Berries Topped with Fresh Whipping Cream

◆

Smoked Salmon and Cream Cheese or Really Great Exotic Cheese on Black Bread

◆

Toasted English Muffin topped with Peanut Butter and Honey

◆

Warm Croissants with Preserves

◆

A Toasted Bagel with Herbed Cream Cheese

◆

Seriously Sumptuous Fruit, Peeled and Eaten with Your Fingers

◆

Freshly Squeezed Fruit Juice

Maria's Adieu

*S*ometimes the morning after just doesn't seem to hold the same rosy glow of the night before. For those occasions, my dear friend Maria recommends keeping a stash of lidded Styrofoam cups on hand. Offering a freshly brewed cup of coffee, packed up to go, surely makes a statement. Adieu!

Seduction Scenarios

MENUS TO MAKE THE MOOD

Turn seduction into performance art as you act out your favorite fantasy with menus to match your sensual mood.

A Valentine's Day Seduction Menu

This holiday designed for lovers, inspired by Cupid, deserves a lavish menu, replete with aphrodisiacs and sensual foods. Pull out the crystal, silver, and china to make these dishes look truly elegant. Champagne would be the perfect way to toast your lover, and a robust cabernet sauvignon would be an intense match for the main course.

Oysters with Apple Mignonette

◆

Radicchio, Rose Petal and Pomegranate Salad

◆

Baked Salmon with Raspberry Cabernet Sauce
Or
Steak Au Poivre with Pink Peppercorns

◆

Sugar Snap Peas with Pearl Onions

◆

Seductive Chocolate Soufflés

◆

ROMANZA DI ITALIA

*P*ut on your favorite Andrea Boccelli music, uncork a bottle of Chianti and succumb to the romance of Italy.

Grilled Country Bread Perfumed with Virgin Olive Oil and Garlic
Artichokes with Warm Vinaigrette

◆

Wild Wild Mushroom Pasta
Or
Pasta Puttanesca

◆

Cappuccino Tiramisu

◆

Espresso

A TOREADOR'S RED MENU

*D*rink a bottle of rioja. Dress up in tights, a bullfighter's cap and a cape. Tease and tantalize with these Spanish recipes. The red visuals will transform you into a matador and your lover into a raging bull

Grilled Bread with Tomato

Make this easy tapa:
Toast 2 slices of sourdough or French bread.
Rub with olive oil, a garlic clove and a halved plum tomato.

◆

Gazpacho d' Amour

◆

Ajo Colorado: *Fish in Red Garlic Broth*

◆

Sausages in Red Wine

◆

Watermelon Granita

AN INDIAN SPICE SEDUCTION

*D*on a sari, drape colorful scarves over the lamps, and burn some incense. Present a finger bowl to your lover and eat this meal sans utensils, using naan, (Indian flat bread) to scoop tastes of these erotically spiced dishes.

Hummus with Roasted Garlic

◆

Cumin Crusted Scallops with Celery Root Puree

◆

Poached Pears in Cardamom Syrup

◆

Chai Masala *Tea*

A Seduction "Quickie"

*S*pend less time in the kitchen and more time with your lover. Everyone loves a quickie.

Mixed Baby Lettuces with Mustard Vinaigrette

♦

Intimate Chicken Piccata
Or
Capellini with Basil Arugula Pesto

♦

Broiled Plums with Lemon Sorbet
Or
Honeydew with Rosemary Syrup

SOLACE AND SEDUCTION

*H*eat up the night with comfort foods.

Fennel, Artichoke Bottom and Asparagus Empanadas

♦

Baked Cod with Shitake Mashed Potatoes and Shitake Sauce

♦

Romantic Rustic Apple Tartlets
Or
Sexy Five-Spice Oatmeal Raisin Cookies

A Late Night Fireside Supper

*C*url up by the fire on your bearskin rug. Groove to tunes by Frank Sinatra or Barry White. Clothing optional. Hot toddies a must.

Scotch Bonnet Blini

◆

Curried Chick Pea and Roasted Pepper Soup

◆

Rustic Fireside Frittata

◆

*Sumptuous Stuffed Strawberries with Mascarpone Cheese
and Dark Chocolate
Or
Lavender Crème Brûlée*

A Decadent Dessert Orgy

Champagne, rose petals and a bed are the only accompaniments needed for this delightful scenario. Let your imagination run wild!

Frozen Green and Red Grapes with Sugar, Lemon Zest and Walnuts

◆

Chocolate Dipped Cherries

◆

Fresh Apple Slices with Homemade Caramel

◆

Freshly Made Whipping Cream

◆

Fresh Strawberries and Orange Segments

◆

Chocolate Syrup

A Bewitching Bedroom Brunch

*S*leep in late. Stay in your birthday suit. Any day can be Sunday.

Mimosas

◆

Scrambled Eggs with Shitake Mushrooms
Or
Ricotta Hot Cakes with Fresh Strawberry Syrup

◆

Fresh Croissants and a Selection of Jams

◆

Hot Coffee

Seduction Staples

Mastering some of the basics helps to perfect the art of culinary courting.

ROASTING PEPPERS: Coat pepper with olive oil and place under broiler. Roast, turning occasionally, until charred and soft, approximately 15 minutes. Remove pepper from broiler and place it in a paper bag. Let rest for 5 minutes. Remove the pepper from the bag, peel off the skin, remove the stem and tear in half. Remove seeds and dice or tear into serving sized pieces. To puree, put in blender and process until smooth.

PURCHASING FRESH SHELLFISH: In clams, mussels and oysters, look for live mollusks with tightly closed shells. If a mussel's shell is open, tap it to see if it snaps shut. If the shell doesn't shut, it means the mollusk is dead and should not be eaten. Shucked oysters should be packed in containers in their own liquor, which should be clear or opalescent, never cloudy or white. Purchase only enough to serve immediately, as shellfish has a limited shelf life. In scallops, look for a pearly, off-white, or pale golden color. Scallops should have a sweet fresh smell; a spoiled scallop smells sulfurous.

TOASTING NUTS: Place nuts on a cookie sheet and toast under broiler, shaking constantly until the nuts become aromatic and light brown, about 2 or 3 minutes. Remove from cookie sheet and cool on a paper towel.

TOASTING SPICES: Place spices in heated sauté pan over a medium flame, toss quickly until spices become fragrant, about 1-2 minutes.

PEELING AND SEEDING TOMATOES: To peel tomato, submerge it in boiling water for about a minute, and then plunge in ice water. Remove blistered skin with a paring knife. To seed, cut the tomato in half and gently squeeze out the seeds.

ROASTING GARLIC: Heat oven to 400°. Pull the papery husks from the garlic head. Remove the top of a head of garlic with a knife, cutting just enough to expose the interior of each garlic clove. Drizzle lightly with olive oil and wrap tightly in an aluminum foil square. Roast in oven for about 45 minutes

SEEDING CHILE PEPPERS: Rubber gloves are recommended when handling hot peppers, but you can handle them with your bare hands with caution. To seed a chili pepper, cut in half and remove the seeds and white pith with a metal ½ teaspoon measuring spoon. To dice a pepper, make a series of lengthwise slices, leaving one end intact. Cut across the short end of the pepper for a neat, even dice.

FRESH WHIPPING CREAM: Use a wire whisk in a chilled bowl. Add to a ½ cup of heavy cream one teaspoon powdered sugar and ½ teaspoon pure vanilla extract. Whip until cream becomes stiff, forming peaks when whisk is lifted from the cream.

ZESTING CITRUS FRUITS: With a vegetable peeler, remove the skin of the citrus fruit, avoiding the bitter white pith underneath. Cut into thin strips or dice.

SALT AND PEPPER: Coarse kosher salt and freshly ground black pepper impart the best flavor to most foods.

WINE: Choose a wine that you would like to drink with the meal you're cooking.

Grow an Erotic Herb Garden

Having fresh herbs ready for snipping is a luxury everyone can share. Purchase seedlings from your local nursery. Plant them in clay pots, a window box, the earth or tend to them in their simple plastic containers. For cooking, you'll love the fresh flavor and fragrance they impart. For instant sensual pleasure, run your fingers among their foliage, inhale their scents and dream of all the tantalizing dishes you'll create.

Here are some erotically appealing herbs:

BASIL: Used as an ancient love charm, basil's pungent flavor enhances almost any dish.

CILANTRO: The bold leaves of the coriander seed, a truly provocative offspring of the seed used in ancient love potions.

DILL: In sixteenth-century England the seeds of dill were believed to stimulate desire. The feathery leaves impart zest to a myriad of dishes and make an excellent garnish for soups and fish.

LAVENDER: Small doses of lavender are rumored to arouse a dream-like state. The fragrance is both stimulating and soothing. Both the flowers and the leaves add intrigue to sweet and savory dishes.

MINT: The Arabs have always believed that mint enhances virility and modern herbalists prescribe it for cases of impotence and decreased virility. Sweet-smelling mint shines in salsas, beverages, and desserts.

PARSLEY: Enjoys a long tradition as an aphrodisiac and as a cook's staple in stocks, soups and garnishing.

ROSEMARY: Medieval women bathed in its fragrance to allure men and offered gilded twigs to wedding guests. The Romans touted rosemary as an amatory stimulant. Don't be afraid to use it lavishly, as it grows like a weed, and a seedling can become a hedge within a month.

SAGE: The fragrance of this herb carries a lusty, earthy undertone reminiscent of Tuscan hillsides and cozy nights by the fire. Fry whole leaves in butter to create an easy and delicious appetizer. Or add to a bath combined with rosemary, thyme, bay leaves, and cloves to relax and inspire.

THYME: Dioscorides, the first century Greek physician, wrote of thyme's ability to excite the senses. Thyme has been called an assertive and brazen herb, qualities that translate well in many seductive scenarios.

Recipe Index

About the Author

DIANE BROWN is a restaurant-industry pro-
fessional and proprietor of Intimate Cater-
ing. In addition to serving romantic meals
to thousands of happy couples, she teaches
aphrodisiac cooking classes. Her recipes can
be found in *Gourmet, Bon Appetit, Sunset* and
Love magazines.

Diane resides in Los Angeles, California.